Bonded in Battle
Vietnam—June 29, 1966

Captain Jack T. Kelley
Commanding Officer
A Company, 2nd Bn, 503rd Infantry
173rd Airborne Brigade

Bonded in Battle: Vietnam…June 29, 1966
Copyright © 2018 Jack T. Kelley

Printed in the United States of America

Developmental editing by Chuck Dean
173rd Airborne Brigade (Sep) 1964-1966
http://www.amazon.com/author/chuckdeanbooks

Cover Photographs:
(a) Sgt Charles Morris—Medal of Honor recipient.
(b) The survivors of 3rd Platoon after the battle.

Foreword

I am honored to have been asked to pen the foreword for *"Bonded in Battle"*. It's a riveting narrative written by my good friend, and Citadel classmate, Jack Kelley who courageously led the men of Alpha Company, 2nd Battalion, 503rd Airborne Infantry of the 173rd Airborne Brigade during the battle of Xuan Loc, Vietnam in June, 1966.

Before I introduce this book to the reader, I want you to know that I am but a humble US Air Force pilot, who was privileged to fly close air support missions as an F-4C aircraft commander and flight leader during my combat tour with the 12th Tactical Fighter Wing at Cam Ranh Bay Air Base, Vietnam from March of 1968 to March of 1969. I flew in support of our Army ground units as well as Marine units in all four corps areas as well as interdiction missions in Laos and North Vietnam. I did so without knowing a lot about the choreography of ground maneuver. It wasn't until I read this book, did I realize how little I did know. I understood, "two up, one back, hot meals and dry socks", but that was about it. I could always hit the forward air controller's smoke with pretty good accuracy, which I hoped helped the "good guys".

The most rewarding missions I flew were when our troops were in direct combat with the enemy. What this narrative accurately portrays are the horrid conditions of jungle warfare, while facing a determined enemy and the agony of seeing comrades being wounded and die on the battle field and the super human strength and superb leadership, which maintained unit cohesiveness, which ultimately prevailed over that determined enemy. The sheer courage of these airborne soldiers that Jack led in this prolonged gun fight Xuan Loc was absolutely astonishing—but not surprising. They were simply the best airborne soldiers following in a great long line going back to WWII.

The format of this book is most helpful, in that Jack has woven in what was happening two command echelons above his Alpha Company and below, down to the squad level. The personal accounts and statements of the battle's survivors really pull the narrative together to give the reader a clear picture of the entire event. Believe me, Alpha Company earned every award and decoration presented to them, especially the Medal of Honor awarded to Sergeant Charles Morris. What a hell of a soldier!

The privilege of penning this Foreword has made me feel a lot better about the role I played some two years after this battle. To Jack and his men, I thank you for your service and sacrifice. To those who pick up this book, enjoy the read and be proud of your fellow Americans who served in Vietnam!

E.G. "Buck" Shuler, Jr.
Lt. General, USAF, Retired
Former Commander of Eighth Air Force
March 1988 to MAY 1991

Table of Contents

Acknowledgements

For so many years June 29, 1966 has been on my mind. It was a time and place that changed all of our lives; and the encompassing details of the battle on that day will never to be forgotten. Such events transpired near Xuan Loc, Vietnam while I was the Company Commander of Alpha Company, 2nd Battalion, 503rd Airborne Infantry of the 173rd Airborne Brigade. During that battle recounted here I fought alongside some of the bravest paratroopers in the U.S. Army.

Along with the help of a number of those men who shared that day with me, the following story is an attempt to re-capture that time, place, and memories. My thanks to them and so many others that contributed to this project—especially to those who kept me on course. To Bev Guy, my strong right arm for her composition and page layout. Lou "Smitty" Smith, the Editor of the 2nd Battalion, 503rd Airborne Newsletter, for all his support. To Col. Ken Smith, for his encouragement and oversight. Mike Thibault for his insight and the documentation on Sgt. Charles Morris, a recipient of the Medal of Honor. To the 1st Bn, 505th Airborne Infantry for their help in developing sketches of the battlefield. Thanks to Marie Carpenti of the National Archives Records Administration (NARA) who steered me in the search for the needed information. Also to Bill Palmer (who answered a 1000 questions), as well as Jim Healy. They never left their posts in encouraging me to complete the story. As you read through my thoughts I want you to know that they are flowing through–with much correction and help–from the pen of my Editor, and fellow Skysoldier, Chuck Dean.

In all of this I want to salute and recognize my sons, Jack Jr. and Shawn. It was Shawn's idea for the project and I thank him for his skill, drive, and patience that saw it completed. Then too, he also forced his brother Jack Jr. to tag along and help and we went to Ft Benning, Oklahoma City and Alexandria, VA. Finally, to my wife Lynn, for not "leaving or forsaking me" while the project was being done.

Now if I could–and I realize I can't–I would ask each of you to close your eyes and imagine that you are crawling inside of me just for that one day. You would see the things that I and my troops saw and felt, touched, and experienced just as they happened. In fact, I would ask that after you have walked through this book with me that you try to feel you were with us; and if you do, that makes you a special part of Company A. Welcome aboard...let's move out!

"Clem Green"

"Clem Green" was a term of endearment used to describe the average, everyday, mythical, hardworking and downtrodden paratrooper infantryman who bore the brunt of every battle—and the mistakes of leadership. He served as an example to everyone of what to do. There was a sign posted near the entrance to "A" Company at the 2/503d's Camp Zinn in Vietnam that proudly announced to all visitors: "Welcome to Alpha Company–Home of Clem Green".

It was the goal of each officer and non-commissioned officer in A Company to try and ensure that the Clem Greens of our company were the best trained and informed paratroopers of the 173rd Airborne Brigade. Combat is a learning experience and one of the key goals of leadership was always to try and ensure that Clem had everything he needed to fight and survive. If the equipment was not on hand, or the supplies were slow in coming, it was not the fault of these young soldiers who deserved the very best...it was ours.

Please remember who he was as you join us in this study of "Clem" on that one specific day, June 29th, 1966. It was a day when leaders were key, and amazingly operated above their assigned position to become the norm. Throughout the company, men moved up and filled positions of higher rank; and did it in a praiseworthy manner. Men with the rank of Sp4 would become squad leaders. Squad leaders would assume the job of Platoon Sergeants, and Platoon Sergeants would become Platoon Leaders.

From my viewpoint, over the following 20 years of military service (mostly in airborne units), my most vivid remembrance was that day, June 29, 1966. It was truly a rare glimpse of such greatness in the conduct and spirit of that young soldier–*PFC Clem Green*. He was, is, and always will be the best.

Additionally, as you follow the steps of "Clem Green" on June 29th, you will quickly become aware that this book is a rare, yet detailed, look at the performance of one soldier, Sergeant Charles Morris. It is the account of how Sergeant Morris became a historical figure–a true American hero. His actions went beyond the call of duty that day as he led his men with courage and bravery; actions that earned him the prestigious Medal of Honor. I think you will agree that he was a genuine "Clem Green".

Airborne!
Jack T. Kelley

Operation Yorktown

It was the wet season and the grey clay sucked hard at our every step—making it difficult to keep our boots on. Ravines swollen with monsoon rain made it slow going, and the dense fog settling over the triple canopy jungle east of Xuan Loc made it a friend to the hundreds of Viet Cong hiding there. We were sent to find them.

Such was the beginning of a day that we brothers-in-arms, paratroopers of A Company, 2nd Battalion, 503rd Infantry, 173rd Airborne Brigade, will never forget; nor will the worthy enemy combatants of the 308th Viet Cong Main Force Battalion. It was June 29, 1966 and a time for those who had never been tested to be tested. I was the Commander of A Company, 2/503d Infantry, and to this day, feel very honored to have served with such first-class fighting men.

Our Company sat on the horizon of an exceptional time in military history as we prepared for Operation Yorktown; which commenced on the 23rd of June in Xuan Loc Province—approximately 37 miles east of Bien Hoa, Vietnam. Initially, the Brigade met only sporadic resistance; however, on the 29th of June, three of our platoons in Alpha Company became engaged with a large enemy force, and the ensuing battle went to a new level.

It is very real to me that a commander is only as good as those he commands. He can be the most proficient leader in the world but if those under his guidance and authority do not

11

perform their duties as trained; his leadership will be of no avail. I was blessed to be surrounded by so many of those well-trained and dedicated warriors during Operation Yorktown. They diligently got the job done; and some even went beyond the call of those duties to ensure victory and demonstrated an immense sacrifice to inspire and protect the lives of those they fought with.

During Operation Yorktown on June 29, 1966 I had the rare opportunity of being present while a Medal of Honor, (the United States of America's highest and most prestigious military decoration awarded for valor to U.S. military members, was being earned). Rarely does the broad general public ever get a chance to learn all the fine details of such an experience. They watch the Presidential presentation on television, see it in the news, and perhaps read the citation statement that describes the heroic account. Few are ever privileged to know more. What more is there to know? This is the question that is answered in this book.

How many accounts of Medal of Honor heroism have ever been described through the eyes and memories of the numerous "Clem Greens" that served alongside that hero? What would it be like to hear detailed testimonials from those brothers-in-arms engaged in the same combat scenario? What they saw, thought, and felt while the intense drama was unfolding? This book provides that rare glimpse.

It has been more than fifty years since Operation Yorktown, and all this time I have carried with me the events thinking that they would simply depart with me when this life is over. Better plans, however, have been laid by mice and men. The insistence and persistence of close family and friends have made sure this story gets told.

A Ride with My Son

The birth of **"Bonded in Battle"** began January of 2016 when I invited my son, Shawn, to accompany me to a conference at the Billy Graham Retreat in the mountains of North Carolina. It was about a two and half hour car ride up there. As he drove us towards the western part of the state I carried the conversation and asked many questions him about his current life; his wife; his kids; his job; and how the advertising agency work was going. My questions and ongoing discussion kept up for the majority of the next couple of hours.

A few days later during our drive back, I once again started with a string of similar questions and he cut me off with, "Dad, we talked about me the whole way up here. Let's talk about you now." Cutting to the chase he then asked, "Tell me about your twenty years in the Army, beginning with graduating from the Citadel and entering the Army as a second Lieutenant. Then tell me everywhere you were stationed, and what your role was until you retired as a Lt. Colonel". It was then that a new journey began for both of us as I told my story.

There was plenty that Shawn knew about the years after I retired because he was in high school at the time, but during the next two and half hours of me sharing, we both realized there was much he didn't know. I told him all that I could remember of my Vietnam service; sharing memories about the Company and its platoons and squads—but most importantly, about the men. When it came to the troops his interest level rose to a new level and seemed to take on a new life.

Soon afterwards our trip Shawn purchased a new DSLR camera that could also shoot high definition video. He asked to interview me on video about my time in Vietnam; clarifying that he wanted to preserve a bit of history to share with family and friends. During the interview he asked me to talk about a specific battle I was involved in during Operation Yorktown. Like some of my military career–he only knew bit and pieces of that story. It became a complete game changer for him. Very soon into the recording of my interview Shawn's keen perception told him that there was much more to this project than just a short video for friends and family. He was right; there was. It has now become a high quality full documentary about a fading memory of American history.

A few months later, I spoke with Shawn and invited him to join me at the annual 173rd Airborne reunion at Fort Benning, Georgia that was on the horizon. I also encouraged him to bring along his video equipment so he could perhaps talk to some of the men who were in Alpha Company at the time of the battle of June 29, 1966.

It was at that point Shawn challenged me to put in writing what we had talked about. Write a book! Once I understood what he was seeking, and why, the project caught fire. He then proposed that while he was attending the annual reunion of the 173rd at Benning that perhaps he could film/record some of the men who were with me as they gave testimony of the battle on June 29-30 1966. He thought the video could blend with the story that I was to write.

His goal was to get inside of each person giving their testimony, and to see/hear their memory of those two days as to how they got to the battlefield, what they saw and did, and what happened to the men around them. It sounded good so in June 2016 we packed our personal gear in my car and loaded his van with the equipment for lighting, filming, and capturing the audio. It soon became a family affair as Shawn talked his brother, Jack Jr., into going along to help out.

The plan came together, and those same testimonies are an integral part of the following narrative of this book. The documentary film, "My Father's Brothers," is a composite view of seven members of Company A who were in the battle of June 29, 1966. (https://www.myfathersbrothers.com/)

Their statements, coupled with battle scenes and audio, places the reader on the ground with these troopers. It's a vivid picture of the individual soldier in combat and of Sgt. Charles Morris..

Far from Fiction

Watching Shawn's excitement prompted me even more to roll up my sleeves and go to work getting as many facts pinned down that I could. Over the next six months I corresponded with the National Archives Records Administration (NARA) and asked for the (a) 2nd Battalion, 503rd Infantry Duty Officer Daily logs (these were daily journals that recorded each contact by phone, radio, or messenger that occurred between our Battalion Headquarters above us and our company, for the dates of the battle, (b) the same information from the 173rd Airborne Brigade, (c) the Lessons Learned from the III Corps After Action Reports, (d) the Morning Reports for the Company for the period June 28, 1966 - July 5, 1966 from the National Personnel Records Center (NPRC) in St. Louis, Mo. (e) and last but not least, the packet of materials that were submitted to recommend Sergeant Charles Morris for the Medal of Honor—our nation's highest military decoration

With this information at hand I had laid the foundation for this story. The key ingredient to the project, of course, was to be able to capture the story of those parachute infantrymen who fought the battle of June 29, and who still come together from time to time to share their lifetime bonding.

The Duty Officer's Log lays out the timeline for each event that took place on June 29, 1966. It is how it actually happened according to verified reports. Within that time line are the stories, memories, doubts and challenges that those soldiers faced on that day. I firmly believe that as you walk with us on that day you will not see one man tell the same exact story, or express the same concerns or challenges. Rather, this telling of June 29th will reveal different personalities, backgrounds-cultural and educational, and a look into their hopes and fears. They were both volunteers and draftees, and a cross section of these United States, except for one thing—they had all volunteered to be paratroopers.

Going to an annual reunion of a combat military unit is not the same as gathering again with friends from high school, or college. Here, the stories will often turn to the loss of a buddy, the sacrifice of one soldier to protect the lives of his fellow squad members, or something unexpected occurring that wasn't planned. I am sure that at a high school or college reunion there are vivid memories, but I cannot believe that anything compares to revisiting a battle and recalling what each person did and thought that day; and what they felt, experienced, and hoped. For me it was, and still is, also a significant time to not only remember, but continue to be in prayer for those with whom we served, those that fell on the battlefield, and those that we have lost in the years since June 29, 1966. Looking back, it seems that I was in the wrong place, at the wrong time, but with the right guys. We were, and have certainly become, a band of brothers.

To my amazement, and as an added note of interest, the timeframe of when we began working to prepare this packet it was almost a week, to the day, that we had engaged ourselves in that battle in Vietnam 50 years prior.

No, this narrative is not one of fiction. What you will read here are the stories that some of the men walked through on that day; how they felt, reacted, and completed the task that they had been assigned. Their impressions lay out what happened that day, and I know each story, statement, and remembrance to be true, because I was there.

For some added clarification this book is basically laid out in five parts: Part One deals with elements and timeline in which the story unfolds. Part Two shows the 2d Battalion, 503d Infantry's Duty Officer's Log Report, and combines statements by our soldiers as they were experienced. Part Three is a recap of the casualties and awards that the company experienced and received for that day. Part Five is a specific and detailed look at what one soldier, Sgt Charles B. Morris did on that day that would have his country recognize him with the Medal of Honor, our nation's highest military decoration.

These five vital parts all come together as they deal with one day—June 29th, 1966. They all focus on one unit in the United States Army—Company A, 2nd Battalion, 503rd Airborne Infantry of the 173rd Airborne Brigade. These five parts merge and culminate bringing together a special story of what individual soldiers of Company A experienced on that date.

Part One
Elements & Timeline

This is a recounting of the battle by Company A, 2nd Battalion, 503rd Infantry on June 29-30, 1966 with the 308th Viet Cong Main Force Battalion. It uses as a foundation the 173rd Airborne Brigade's Daily Staff Journal or Duty Officer's Log and primarily the 2d Bn, 503d's Daily Staff Journal or Duty Officer's Log, Staff Officer's Log for those communications between the Battalion and Co A.

Throughout the Log input, wherever another item of information is needed to fill out the story of that day, the information is inserted and footnoted or displayed as an attachment. These come from (a) the Brigade Operations Order and its Addendums - e.g. the Intelligence Addendum, (b) fourteen witness statements taken from those posted June 29 (a number of these attended the reunion at Ft. Benning, Georgia and had their reports taped for Shawn's documentary), (c) those eleven witness statements taken from the Sgt Morris Medal of Honor Packet (MOH) was furnished by the National Archives & Records Administration (NARA), and from the National Personnel Records Center in St Louis.

Several special reports have also been included as well as one by Capt. Coker from the 173d Airborne Brigade Headquarters based on his interview with 3rd Platoon members that were WIA on June 29th, and a report by Capt John Boykin,

S-2 of the 2d Bn, 503d Infantry that has been taken from the Medal of Honor (MOH) packet on Sgt Charles Morris and inserted to add focus to the narrative. National Archive and Records Administration (NARA) supplied the witness statements that are included in the Sgt Morris MOH section, the maneuver sketches of the company and the 3rd platoon, as well as lists of the 3d Platoon KIAs and Awards. Two additional sketches were produced by the 1st Battalion, 505th Airborne Infantry—the Company A Maneuver Plan and the 2d Battalion Airmobile Plan. The goal here is to use the 2d Battalion, 503d Abn Infantry Battalion Duty Officer Log as the foundation and the information mentioned above to provide actuality and continuity.

Finally, at Ft Benning, we filmed/recorded those witness statements of those present and blended them with the above to make a documentary of Company A on June 29th-30th, 1966. Even though many of the statements that focus on the entire narrative are based on my recollection of the events, I am also aware that each of those in Company A who were involved may have a variety of views of what they saw, heard, and believed happened.

The Combat Operations

As with all combat operations it is advantageous to gather an overall all picture of the battlefield, its conditions, the enemy, our friendly forces and their mission. For the purpose of making an accurate recounting these elemental materials hereon have been generously borrowed from the OPORDs our Battalion and the Brigade that have references prior. The following information of Company A on each hour of June 29 and 30 will give the reader a better view and understanding as to what these paratroopers faced, what they did, and why they did it during that timeframe.

Pausing a moment, allow me to ask you to consider the following as you read these next few sections. Although one might sense that reading about "Terrain, Weather, and Enemy" that they are just here for a fill-in; however, I would hope to assure you that these three elements greatly impacted my soldiers on that day—big time! The weather caused the rain and mud to greatly hinder our movement to the enemy and significantly held us back from reaching the 3rd Platoon when they attacked the 308th Viet Cong Main Force Battalion. Then too, the terrain was also a determent to movement, and observation. The enemy, the 308th Battalion, was a professional force that greatly outnumbered us. In hind sight, combining all of these; weather, terrain, and enemy; made for one great challenge.

A. The Terrain

The area was characterized by rolling hills with an elevation of between 100 and 200 meters, with stream filled ravines, dense rain forests and jumble. Generally, there were two/three canopy coverings, providing good concealment from ground and air observation and partial cover from direct fire weapons. Cross-country movement for foot troops was good, except in rain, forest and jungle covered areas where movement was poor and clay was a real problem. June and July were wet season, and rainfall increased through that period.

We were informed that terrain would have an effect on the enemy in that they would make maximum use of concealment afforded by vegetation to cover their maneuver.

For many in the company this was the first experience they had with a dense jungle environment. The "two/three canopy" we encountered made it difficult to receive airdrops, helicopter re-supply, directing of air strikes and communications with higher headquarters. A number of witness statements attest to the fact that there was much water on the landing zone and throughout the area of operations. In certain areas movement was hindered by the ground being water-soaked. Additionally, several platoons would report that grey mud was in front of every step beginning at the Landing Zone till the objectives were reached; movement was significantly slowed through that period.

B. The Weather

Surface wind gusts from thunderstorms can reach as high as 50 knots. The wind is calm 29 per cent of the time during June. Cloudiness increases over the objective area during June. Average precipitation would be 9.4 inches. Nighttime cloudiness continues to increase at middle and high levels. The average maximum temperature during June is 89 degrees and the average minimum temperature is 75 degrees. The average relative humidity is 82 percent.

Effect on Enemy Courses of Action: During periods of low visibility, rain and fog, the VC was afforded relative freedom of movement without observation.

Effect of Friendly Courses of Action: During periods of cloudiness and low visibility friendly use of tactical air was restricted; as were helicopters.

C. The Enemy - Three tier VC military formation:

The Viet Cong/Peoples Liberation Armed Forces (VC/PLAF) military formations were generally grouped into 3 echelons.

- *VC Main-Force Units.* The elite of the VC were the *chu luc* or Main Force Units, made up of full-time fighters. These units generally reported to one of the Interzone headquarters or were controlled directly by Central Office of South Vietnam (COSVN). Many of the soldiers were southern-born and had been trained in the north before re-infiltrating back to serve the Revolution. A majority of main-force fighters were party members, wore the pith helmet common to the NVA, carried the same weapons, and could operate in battalion or even regimental size strengths. A typical battalion was similar to a NVA one, with 400–600 men organized into 3 infantry companies backed by a fire support company. Recon, signals, sapper and logistics units rounded out the formation.

- *The Regional Forces.* Regional or territorial units were also full-time soldiers but they generally served within or close to their home provinces. They did not have the degree of literacy of the main-force personnel, and did not have the percentage of Party members present in their ranks. They were not as well armed as the *chu luc* and usually operated in units that seldom exceeded company strength.

- *Village Guerrillas.* Village, hamlet or local guerrillas were part-time fighters and helpers, carrying out minor harassment operations like sniping or mine/booby trap laying, building local fortifications or supply caches, and transporting supplies and equipment. Mostly peasant farmers, these militia style units were under the control of low level NLF or Front leadership.

- *Transitions.* Although manpower shortages sometimes intervened, a hierarchical promotion system was generally followed between the 3 levels. Promising guerrilla level operatives were moved up to the Regional Forces, and promising Regional Force fighters were promoted to the full-time Main Force units. This ensured that the Main Forces received the best personnel, with some seasoning under their belts.

From OPOR (Operations Order) 19-66 we were told that the enemy situation consisted of two guerrilla companies that were operating in the area to the south of Xuan Loc. The D 82d Local Force Battalion was probably located in northern Long Khanh Province. Elements of the 274th Regiment may be located west of Courtenay Plantation, but more likely they were in the Hat Ditch area. The strength of the enemy was a well-established intelligence net in the area. The VC was thoroughly familiar with the area and the terrain was well suited for individual and small unit tactics.

The enemy force we encountered was the 308th Viet Cong Main Force Battalion of the 274th Viet Cong Regiment (AKA 4th Dong Nai Regiment), which had three battalions, and eight support companies; (82mm mortars, 12.7 Machine Gun, 75 mm Recoilless Rifles, Commo, Transportation, and Engineer). The regiment was thought to have 1,500 men recruited from outside the area, supplemented by NVA, regional and local VC elements that acted as scouts. The average VC Main Force Battalion would have the strength of 350. The

Regiment consisted of about 1,500 men recruited from outside the area of operations, supplemented by North Vietnamese Army regulars. Local Viet Cong elements acted as scouts during operations. It was part of the VC 5th Main Force Division 10,000 strong, North Vietnamese Army (NVA). The unit, the 308th, was also known as the D3 Bn, the K-3 or the 3rd Bn of the 274th VC MF Regiment. Documents also indicated the C-11 Company was in this action. The 308th, according to organizational documents reviewed, consisted of a Headquarters, three rifle companies, and a heavy weapon company. This follows the "system of 3" in the VC organization. There would be three men in a cell, three cells in a squad, three squads in a platoon, three platoons in a company and three companies in a battalion. Additionally, the company would have a Heavy Weapons Platoon and that unit would contain 82mm mortars, Recoilless Rifles and Heavy Machine guns.

In describing the enemy units there would often be a difference in personnel and equipment. For instance, in personnel our Battalion S-2 Intelligence Officer estimated the 308th was a force of 100 plus–other units operating that we have records of, show a Battalion being of a larger a force e.g., the 267 MF Bn (25% NVA) was at 450. The D445 Battalion that fought the Aussies (Australian Army units) at Long Tan on August 18th, 18 days after our battle with the 308th MF battalion had the strength of 350. This would be the Australian Army's most costly engagement. The 38th Independent Bn was at the strength of 300, and the Phu Loi Battalion II had a strength of 500 a year later. Records from the battle of Hue show a typical VC MF Bn at 300-600. From a review of data obtained on the internet on Viet Cong forces of Battalion level, it appears the average VC MF Battalion had the strength of 350.

27

In hindsight, it appears to this participant of the battle that our 3rd Platoon attacked a much larger enemy force than was thought to be there. Additionally, when we list enemy weapons such as the recoilless rifle–we found casings for both the 75mm and the 57mm regardless of what VC documents indicate would be found at Battalion level. Major Battles that the 274th would be engaged in were Suoi Chau Phs, Hat Ditch, Long Khah, and Phouc Long. The 308th VC Main Force Bn was a guerrilla unit until 1976 when it was designated as a regular unit stationed in Hat Ditch. In 1969 it left the 274th and became known as the K-3 of the NVA.

The enemy weapons that we encountered, along with their type, number and location, are included in Table 1 below. The information is based on reports listed in the above. NARA packet. The 308th main force battalion was organized in two defensive positions.

Table 1 Weapons Encountered

Weapons	Position #1	Position #2
50 cal machine guns	2	1
30 cal machine guns	3	2
60 mm mortars	1	1
57/75 mm Recoilless Rifle	3	1
Assault weapons	50	30
.5 Rocket Launcher	2	1

*Weapons that we encountered consisted of mortars 60mm or 82mm mortars, 30 cal and 50 cal machine guns, as well as several 57mm and 75mm recoilless rifles, and AK47 rifles. Capt. Coker's and A Company both reported on the 30th that both 57mm and 75mm casings were found. Additionally, we were faced with 12.7mm antiaircraft machine guns.

Enemy capabilities: The Brigade Operations Order 9-66 and Bn Order 19-66 stated: The enemy could attack initially with guerrilla forces located of Xuan Loc and reinforce with elements of the 274th and 275th Regiments. An attack, if made, would be by main force units moved into the area. Any major attack would be of short duration at a time and place that the enemy felt tactical surprise could be achieved in order to avoid heavy losses from air and artillery fire. The enemy would not defend with larger than squad size forces...feeling that to do so would cause heavy casualties from superior firepower.

In our battle the enemy did defend but it was felt that this might be because it appeared that only a small force, the 3rd Platoon, was being engaged. The conclusion of the Intelligence Estimate was that the most probable enemy course of action will be that of harassment and small scale ambushes to inflict maximum casualties on friendly forces. When the rest of the company began to close on the enemy force they begin to withdraw.

Since our company was attacking an enemy force we should look at the enemy's defensive tactics. (The following description of the enemy and his tactics are largely taken from the Intelligence Annex of the Brigade Operations Orders, Wikipedia on Vietcong tactics and Wikipedia on the 275th VC Main Force Regiment).

Defensive tactics

VC/NVA defensive doctrine generally stressed avoidance of extended battle. Unless an enemy sweep or patrol provoked an engagement, communist forces generally lay low until they were ready to initiate their own actions. If an engagement ensued, the typical approach in terms of defense was to delay opposing forces and withdraw as soon as possible, while inflicting maximum casualties before withdrawal.

A key part of the avoidance defensive pattern also involved the intensive use of fortifications and mines. Both served to enable Front forces to escape for another day's fighting, while running up the enemy tab in blood and treasure.

Defensive positions had to be prepared every time VC/NVA troops moved to a new destination, with an eye to the suitability of terrain, camouflage and withdrawal routes. Generally a two line system of fortifications was used, about 50–200 meters apart. The lines were typically shaped like an L, U or V to enhance interlocking fields of fire. Individual L-shaped fighting positions were also dug, with bunkers at right angles covered with thick logs and about 2 feet of dirt. Shallow trenches connected many individual bunkers and positions into each belt of the 2-line system. The bunkers provided cover from inevitable US artillery and air attack, and the fighting positions allowed crossfire against infantry assaults. The second line of defense was not visible from the first line of positions, and allowed the fighters to fall back, either to escape a heavy bombardment, to continue retreating or to furnish a rallying point for counterattack.

In some circumstances front fortifications did not follow the layout scheme described above. Bunkers and fighting holes were scattered more widely to delay attackers, and create the psychological impression that they were surrounded on all sides. Lookout posts were often positioned on key trails, routes and likely US helicopter landing zones. To enhance their mobility during a defensive battle, numerous air-raid shelters, bunkers and trenches were pre-built in advance around an area of operations. This involved an enormous amount of labor but proved their value in maneuvering under Army Republic of Vietnam (ARVN)/US attacks. Foxholes dug by VC troops during the victorious Battle of Ap Bac are testimony to the insurgents almost religious dedication to field fortifications. The holes were dug so deep that a man could stand inside. Excavation of dirt was from the rear, hiding telltale traces of the digging. Only a direct hit by an artillery shell or bomb could kill troops inside such holes. Behind the line of foxholes, the Viet Cong utilized and improved an irrigation ditch, allowing them concealed movement, communication and transmission of supplies on foot or by sampan. Most of these fighting positions were invisible from the air.

Hugging techniques, timings, counterattacks and withdrawal:

The VC/NVA fighters sought to neutralize US and ARVN firepower by "hugging" enemy troops—fighting so close that artillery or aircraft strikes had to be restrained for fear of friendly fire casualties. Vigorous counterattacks were also made, particularly against weaker ARVN formations. Typically, VC/NVA troops in a defensive or ambush position held their fire or maneuvered until US troops were very close before opening fire. This initiated the "hug" method. Since their enemies would generally draw back upon contact and rely on supporting fires, front troops moved with them…"hanging on the belt."

Viet Cong Soldiers – Getty Images

Actions against enemy forces were often initiated in the latter part of the day, with impending nightfall providing favorable conditions for withdrawal. When surrounded, the Main Force VC and especially the NVA fought tenaciously, but usually with an eye towards withdrawal. Great efforts were made in recovering bodies, a psychological warfare measure that denied opponents the satisfaction of viewing enemy dead.

There was a withdrawal scheme for all operations whether defensive or offensive. Escape and exit routes were pre-planned and concealed in advance, with later regrouping at a planned assembly point.

We would find out shortly after the battle started that the enemy force was a well-trained main force Viet Cong Battalion with North Vietnamese Army regulars and several Chinese or Manchurian advisors attached.

D. Friendly Forces

In addition to our units from the 173rd ABN, we were also supported by the following:

1. 10th ARVN Div (-) located at Xuan Loc and Gia Ray conducted operations in area adjacent to AO Yorktown.
2. Regional and Provincial units in Xuan Loc sector secured their present locations.
3. 145th Aviation Battalion would support the air assault with 30 slicks and armed helicopters as required.
4. Tactical Air Force was on call.
5. Battery A 2/32nd Arty in general support, reinforcing.
6. 173rd Airborne Brigade. The mission of the 173rd Airborne Brigade-Operation Yorktown-OPORD 9-66: The 173d Abn Bde escorts A 2/32 Arty to Xuan Loc 23 Jun; deployed one battalion to vic XUAN LOC 23 June; follows with one battalions and remainder of forces to vic Xuan Loc o/a 25 Jun; and conducted subsequent operations south east of Xuan Loc to locate and destroy NVA/VC elements. The details of the Bde order included a three-phase operation starting with the movement of forces both by air and road to a forward staging areas for the conduct of the operation. Then in Phase two the 2/503 (our battalion) deployed into the area of operation that has been assigned to the battalion. Phase 3, after June 25 Bde conducted operations to destroy NVA/VC in AO Yorktown. (Actually, the assault, due to weather were delayed until June 29th- at which time the 2d Bn released its three companies and the reconnaissance platoon to conduct operations in their assign AO's)
7. 2d Bn, 503d Abn Inf. The Battalion consisted of three rifle companies and a mortar company and reconnaissance

platoon. We, Company A, was one of those companies. We were one of three companies in the 2d Bn of the 503 Infantry Regiment (Airborne). In addition to the three rifle companies (A, B and C) there was a Mortar Company (consisting of three 81mm mortars) and a Reconnaissance Platoon. In the narrative for this day we will only look at our rifle company, as that's where the battle was on June 29th.

8. The Royal Australian Regiment (RAR) was attached to the 173rd on numerous occasions. It was a professional combat proven force. For additional information the following will be helpful: Vietnam Task: The 5th Battalion, The RAR 1966-67, Mebourne VK. Cassel Australia. Military History of Australia During The Vietnam War, Wikipedia, Vietnam Veterans Association of Australia, Anza House, 4 Collins Street, Melbourne VK 2001.
(www.6rarassociation.com, www.5rarasn.au)

If you were to look into the Army Field Manual (FM 7-11) that described what our company should have looked like, you would find something different on June 29th. We were one of three companies in the 2d Battalion of the 503rd Infantry Regiment (Airborne). In addition to the three rifle companies (A, B, and C) there was a Mortar Company (consisting of three 81mm mortars) and a Reconnaissance Platoon.

A Company consisted of 170 in the field. We had a headquarters element made up of me (the Company Commander), the 1st Sgt, Tony Torres, my two Radio Telephone Operators (RTO), (one carried the Battalion Command net–Sp4 Johnson and the other carried the Company net radio, The there was the Artillery Forward Observer (Lt. Pascaserall) and his RTO, and the Senior Medic–Sp5 Beaton and the Battalion

Chaplain Conrad Walker who was with us that day–Praise The Lord!

We had the three rifle platoons and a weapons platoon. Each of the rifle platoons had a headquarters with a platoon leader, platoon sergeant, a radio telephone operator (RTO), forward observer and a medic. The three squads consisted of a squad leader and 10 men divided into two 5-man fire teams– Alpha and Bravo. They were armed with M-16 rifles and M-79 (40mm) grenade launchers. The Weapons squad would have a squad leader and two teams each carrying an M-60 machine gun. The weapons platoon consisted of a platoon leader, platoon sergeant and radio telephone operator (RTO), and medic. The fire direction center and three mortar squads carried the 81mm mortars.

On June 29, we did have the three rifle platoons. However, two of them were commanded by SSGs (E-6s) instead of Lieutenants. Each of the four platoons were to have a Platoon Sergeant (E-7), but three of the four had as a Platoon Sergeant a SSG (E6) who would have normally commanded a squad. Then the squad leaders–which were supposed to be SSGs (E-6) was Sgts (E-5) holding that position. 1st Platoon was 1st Lt Vose, 2nd Platoon was SSG Brown, 3rd Platoon was SSG Cooney and the Weapons was 1st Lt Vendetti.

E. The Mission of the 2d Battalion (Airborne) 503d Infantry

The 2d Bn (Abn) 503d INF conducted airmobile assault on the following Landing Zones: LZ Brazil (A Company), LZ Peru (B Company) and LZ Chile (C Company), to initiate saturation patrols and ambushes in Area of Operations 4 (AO4). Locate and destroy NVA/VC elements, and were prepared to conduct subsequent operations south on order. The operation was delayed initially for 24 hours due to weather from the 28th to the 29th.

The Battalion's concept of operations to fulfill the mission was that one company was airlifted into each LZ, to secure a company base, deploy platoons and squads to cover the largest possible area with patrols and ambushes. Specific tasking for each unit to execute was as follows:

Team Alpha
Conduct air assault on LZ BRAZIL
Secure patrol base, conduct saturation patrols and ambushes
Subsequently have a platoon force clear Objectives BRAGG (YT 573013) and ORD
Select and prepare extraction LZ
Be prepared to extract o/a 1 July

Team Bravo
Conduct air assault on LZ Chile
Secure patrol base, conduct saturation patrols and ambushes.
Subsequently have platoon force clear Objectives CAMPBELL and LEWIS.
Select and prepare extraction LZ.
Be prepared for extraction o/a 1 July.

Team Charlie
Conduct air assault on LZ PERU
Secure patrol base, conduct saturation patrols and ambushes.
Subsequently have platoon force clear Objectives DIX, POLK and BLISS.
Select and prepare extraction LZ.
Be prepared for extraction o/a July 1
.

Recon Platoon
Secure LZ WHITE NLT 29063H June 66

Fire Support
3d Bn, 319th Artillery supported from LZ RED

Five minute armed helicopter preparation on LZ CHILE, and LZ PERU (No preparation on LZ BRAZIL). TAC air on station during assault.

      The day prior to our launch there was an opportunity to do a recon of the initial entry areas. Taking the Platoon Leaders, we did a recon of the general area by helicopter. It provided us with a view of the landing zone (LZ) we were to land on—LZ Brazil, and the other areas that we were to operate in.
      What this mission statement meant for us in A Company was that once we had landed and assembled, we were to break down by platoons with each covering a portion of the AO (area of operations) assigned to A Company. The rifle platoons were to be 1,000 meters apart as they advanced to the west. In hindsight, this would result in a major problem for the company. We were assigned two initial objects-Bragg and Ord, and then to select and prepare an extraction landing zone (LZ) and be prepared to for extraction o/a 1 July. One item that we were cautioned about in the coordinating instructions was that there would be absolutely NO "scorched earth" actions allowed!
      As each platoon advanced within their sector they had a "point" (several men out in front of the platoon) to provide early warning if there was an enemy force in the front. Also, each platoon had additional security out to each flank and security covering the rear of the platoon as it advanced. At times, the platoon might stop and send a squad out to either flank to check

37

out suspected areas that they might have thought to be enemy positions. The movement of the platoons would be slow, and emphasis would be on stealth and security. In the event any of the security elements were to encounter an enemy force, the Platoon Leader had the option to deploy the remainder of his platoon to engaged the enemy force, stop and defend or call for the Company to reinforce his position or withdraw. Search and destroy encompassed active small recon patrols searching out for possible enemy positions and then a "pile on" by the rest of the unit to overcome the enemy position.

F. Execution

The concept of operations had each of the companies airlifted into its assigned LZ, secure a company base, and deploy its platoons and squads to cover the largest possible area with patrols and ambushes. The Battalion would have fire support from the 3d Bn, 319th Artillery at LZ Red. Additionally a five-minute armed helicopter preparation on LZ Chile and LZ Peru (No preparation on LZ Brazil). Tactical Air on station during the air assault.

Company A was the first company to lift off and conduct its air assault on LZ Brazil and engage in its mission.

Airmobile Operations
29 June, 1966

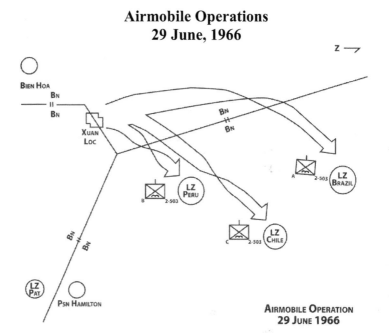

AIRMOBILE OPERATION
29 JUNE 1966

An After Action Summary:

On 29 June 1966, near Xa Xuan Loc, Republic of Vietnam, Company A, 2d Battalion (Airborne) 503d Infantry, seized the Battalion Headquarters of the 308th Main Force Battalion (Viet Cong) after a furious battle. A number of documents were captured by Company A, including an operations plan for an attack on the Army of Vietnam garrison at Xa Gia Ray and the subsequent ambush of the relief column coming from Xa Xuan Loc. When the garrison at Xa Gia Ray came under attack the relief column, now aware of the Viet Cong trap, preceded their movement with an airstrike in the area where the ambush was expected. Upon arrival in the area, they found over 20 dead Viet Cong, this prevented the destruction of the relief column and enabled it to reinforce the beleaguered garrison at Xa Gia Ray. The Viet Cong broke contact at Xa Gia Ray and withdrew. Among the other documents captured by Company A was a diary which described the high rate of malaria in the 308th Main Force Battalion (Viet Cong) and identified other enemy units in the area. A sheet of the current Viet Cong passwords was also captured.

JOHN T. BOYKIN
Captain, Infantry
Battalion S-2

Part Two
Duty Officer Logs and Other Reports

The following are based on (1) entries in both the 2d Bn Daily Staff Journal of Duty Officer's Log and (2) the Daily Staff Journal or Duty Officer's Log of the Brigade as well as the various Addendums of both units and after action reports. Of significant importance is that the entrees of these logs are actual; whereas the flow of the battle and maneuver of the units and their actions are based upon individual testimonies and on my memory

2d Battalion Daily Staff Journal of Duty Officer's Log June 29, 1966

Duty Officer's Log 0125 - A, B, HHC: Recon Platoon-Patrols preparing to move out.

Duty Officer's Log 0155 - A Co commo check

Duty Officer's Log 0300 - Commo check

Duty Officer's Log 0505 - Commo check

Duty Officer's Log 0454 - A Co ambush patrol on the way in.

Duty Officer's Log 0550 - A Co explosion in 1st platoon area possible mortar or claymore. Checking out the clues at this time.

Duty Officer's Log 0600 - A Co two claymore mines activated into our left flank platoon. Device activated about 300 meters from this position on an azimuth of 210 degree. Four causalities–extent of injuries unknown. Time of action 0545 hours.

Pfc Woody Davis, 1st Platoon:

In early morning just before or at dawn, I heard what sounded like a mortar firing from somewhere at the 10 o'clock direction, down the valley from my Listening Post position. A split second later I heard the explosion at the 1st platoon's position. I started firing my M-79 in the direction of the mortar sound. Haynes was on the radio with Lt. Vose immediately. Lt. Vose ran out to the LP and took over the radio to guide Sgt. Showalter's squad to the suspected motor site to check the area. When it was cleared, everyone returned to the tree line to await the medevac for our losses. Sp 4 Felder and Pfc Graves were KIA, and Sp4 Clover, PFC Borgos and Pluckett were WIA. I remember carrying Felder's body to the chopper in a double poncho liner because his arm slipped out from between the opening and hit my leg.

This action is typical of how the best plans are alerted. While we were moving to the pickup zone to be lifted out for the airmobile assault the 1st platoon was hit with mortars as reported above. By the time they had control of the situation the airmobile lifts were inbound and the 1st platoon had to run to get to the landing zone in time for their lift off. Later, after the airmobile assault and reorganization on Landing Zone Brazil the platoon would have to unpack cases of C Rations they had carried on board- and distribute them to platoon members. Stuff happens!

Duty Officer's Log 0620- Fm Co A: Total casualties, 2 walking, 2 KIA, Bde notified.

There was concern initially that we had been hit by mortar from the nearby village. Bn would later indicate that they thought casualties were caused by Claymore mines and grenades.

Duty Officer's Log 0630-Recon has secured LZ White

Duty Officer's Log 0645 - Bn confirmed with the Bde that causalities were 2 WIA liter cases and 2 KIAs.

Duty Officer's Log 0651- Dust-off helicopter departed A Co with causalities.

Duty Officer's Log 0700 - A Co begins movement to LZ White (this is where we will be picked up to move to our area of operations)

LZ White will be the landing zone that will be used for each of the Bn companies to be picked up from for their airmobile assaults into the Area of Operation. Co A will leave from LZ White and land on LZ Brazil, Co B will land on LZ Peru and Co C on LZ Chile. Each company, in turn, will have 30 helos using 10 in each lift to conduct the airmobile operation.

Duty Officer's Log 0709 - A Co departs for LZ Brazil.

Brigade will say that our lift consists of 30 chalks. There are no Battalion Log items entered as to our airmobile assault onto LZ Brazil and also the Brigade notes will state that we had no artillery, air or helicopter prep of the LZ provided as we landed. We were fortunate that when we landed on LZ Brazil, we encountered no opposition and were able to report to higher headquarters that we had a safe "green LZ". On the ground the first elements that landed, seeing there was no enemy opposition immediately threw out green smoke grenades that indicated to the commander, orbiting above and controlling the assault, that there was no opposition and the remaining "lifts" - succeeding helicopters - were safe to continue coming in.

> **Duty Officer's Log 0832** - A Co reports at 0802 hrs they have discovered 16 prone type foxholes oriented to the SE appears they are 3 to 4 days old-Coordinates 596004.
>
> **Duty Officer's Log 0832** - A Co in LZ Brazil.

Once we landed on the Landing Zone (LZ) all platoons moved to west about 300 meters and, by platoon, took up defensive positions in a huge wagon wheel defensive posture. Immediately the platoon leaders and non-commissioned officers began checking their men again to insure we are accounted for, weapons were ready and ammunition available and we were prepared to execute the mission.

A quick check with each of the 4 platoon leaders and the artillery forward observer, and I gave the command to "Move Out"

At this time the 1st, 2d and 3rd platoons begin their movement to their release points (RP). The Weapons Platoon and the Headquarters element remained in place in a perimeter defensive position, and will act as a reserve, if that is needed.

> **Duty Officer's Log 0906** - Explosions at 0545 were definitely 2 claymores and a possibility that a 3rd explosion was a grenade. Approximately 20 meters from our position.

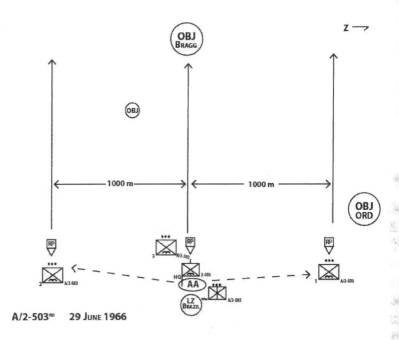

A/2-503ᴿᴰ   29 June 1966

Co A Actual Maneuver Plan – the LZ, Co Assembly Area, the Platoon movement to their Plt Release Points and then their movements west, ending with all platoons on the objective.

Duty Officer's Log 0907- A Co has coordinated with Long Range Recon Patrol (LRRP) element. Element has departed. A Co location: 1st Platoon-590005, 2nd Platoon 596001, 3rd- Platoon 585004, CP & Weapons Platoon-597002

When we landed on LZ Brazil, we moved off the LZ and assembled at a company assembly area to get organized, check commo etc. Once all was ready the platoons were told to move out. The 1ˢᵗ Platoon (1st Lt Vose) was to move to the north 1,000 meters and hold up in a Release Point for further orders.

45

The 2nd Platoon, SSgt Nate Brown, was to move to the south 1,000 meters and hold in a Release Point. The 3d Platoon, SSgt Thomas Cooney, (Lt Larry Allgood, the Platoon Leader was WIA on the 26th and evacuated) was to remain in their initial position until both the 1st and 2nd Platoons were at their release points. Lt. Gus Vendetti, Weapons Platoon, as well as the Headquarters element, were to remain in place until the 1st and 2nd Platoons reached their release points. Once the 1st and 2nd had reached their RP's, I then notified all three rifle platoons to begin moving to the West, conducting saturating patrolling to see if the reported enemy force was in our AO. The Weapons Platoon and the Headquarters element were to remain in position and be ready to act as a reserve if any of the three rifle platoons became engaged with the enemy.

Duty Officer's Log 1012 - Bn commo check

Reviewing what is happening at this time, the three rifle platoons-1st, 2nd and 3rd are moving to the west in what's called a search and destroy operation. They are patrolling very slowly and cautiously looking for the enemy in hope to find, engage and destroy the enemy. The Weapons Platoon and the Company Headquarters are far behind the center platoon, the 3rd platoon, and are prepared to move to support any of the three forward advancing platoons should they become engaged.

As the three rifle platoons are moving to the west they are each moving in a column of two's, every so often their platoon leaders will have them stop and take a rest break, and then, when this occurs the column will stop. The ones on the left side will take a knee and face to the left and the men on the right side will take a knee and face to the right. The platoon leader will also post security - two men to the right from 25 plus meters, depending on the terrain, to provide early warning should the enemy approach the platoon. He will also make sure his point, the front of the column, usually two men, are alert and out to the front. Likewise, at the rear of his platoon–the six o'clock position he will have two men alerted and drop back to provide security there. When the break is over, the platoon leader will give the signal and all security will come in and the platoon will again begin its movement.

This is a standard operating procedure. But in all matters of life problems occur, and one occurred on June 28th the day before our air assault into the battle area. We were moving from an operation we had been on out to the east and were headed to the location where we would spend the night and launch out on the morning of the 29th for our attack. During this move we were in a company column, that is all four platoons were in line and each was in a column of twos. When I had the company stop for a break to rest and then ordered them to move out, the problem occurred. In one of the platoons they had posted their security and when the break ended and the company moved out. As they were moving a young trooper, Specialist 4 Frederic Fritts, went up to his squad leader and informed him that the two left flank security guys had not returned. The squad leader brushed him off thinking that all was well and the platoon and company continued to move. Fritts searched up and down his platoon and failed to find the two soldiers. This time he went to the platoon leader and informed him of the failure of the two flank security men to return. We were still moving. At this time, the platoon leader called me on the radio and informed me. He assured me that he had checked and that they were missing. I stopped the company and ordered them to turn around and head back to where they thought they had placed the two men out on security. We arrived and sent out a fire team of 4-5 men. The team found

47

the men in position along a trail protecting us and…we had walked off and left them

I called the squad leader and took his sergeant stripes off his collar and told him to fall back into the column. I then turned around faced with the task of who to make the squad leader. Back at Camp Zinn, our base camp, we would have had a promotion board and reviewed all the possible candidate's records. But there was no time for that. There stood Fritts. I handed him the stripes and told him he was now a sergeant (and the squad leader) and to look after his men. He did. That night they informed me he checked their equipment and positions and insured all were ready. He was a strong Christian young man and "walked the walk". On the next day when we made our airmobile assault and engaged the enemy, he looked after his squad. He was killed in action that day and posthumously awarded the Silver Star for gallantry in action and the Purple Heart.

Pfc Ron Sedlack, 3rd Plt, Corunna, MI:

As we moved from the assembly area toward the west, Sgt Morris was up front and I was half way back in the column. The first thing I remember was Sgt Morris telling us he had discovered commo wire, then the enemy opened fire with RPGs, MG and Mortars. We were held in place. We could hear the pop of mortars going off. PFC Ball came over to me, he had his weapon shot out of his hand. I had been wounded and he checked me over. He left to check something out but returned. Toward 1:00 we felt movement coming towards us and thought it was the enemy, but it turned out to be the rest of A Company—but we were frightened about it.

Duty Officer's Log 1038 - A Co req Arty fire in cord 580995.

Duty Officer's Log 1035 - (Late Entry) A Co reports 3rd Platoon elements made contact-Enemy Bunker-hit w/50 cal MG-Causalities 2-liter, 1 WIA–unit surrounded –Arty being used.

At this time the other three platoons, 1st, 2d and Weapons were contacted and told to "move to the sound of the guns" as rapidly as possible.

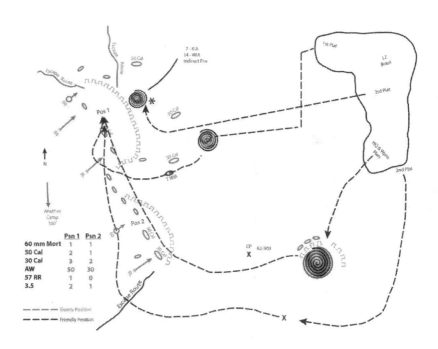

	Psn 1	Psn 2
60 mm Mort	1	1
50 Cal	2	1
30 Cal	3	2
AW	50	30
57 RR	1	0
3.5	2	1

The drawing on the previous page shows the actual maneuver of Co A: the LZ, Co Assembly Area, the Platoon movement to their Plt Release Points, and then their movements west, ending with all platoons on the objective. The drawing is from the Morris Medal of Honor Packet showing the maneuver of Co A on June 29)

Sp 4 Bob Lucas, 2d Plt, East Weymouth, MA:

Upon landing on LZ our Platoon met up with LRRP unit - they had no enemy contact - showed us blue commo wire in tree line. On move out we followed the blue commo wire and eventually heard the gunfire from 3d Plt contact. Seems we moved into an ambush-squad size, and got hit from the rear or flank position. We hit the ground. The enemy element seemed to be protective element of the main force. This slowed us down for about 5-10 minutes. On the radio I heard the CO and passed his message on to SSgt Brown "move to sound of guns.", and we did—on the run and on line. We shortly overran their position and left a squad there. The remainder of the platoon continued on to the 3rd platoon.

Duty Officer's Log 1050 - (Late Entry) A Co reports about 20 VC with 2- 50 cal MG and have received some mortars. No LZ. No dust-off at this time. A Co receiving all Arty needed—doing fine.

Duty Officer's Log 1123 - A Co reports 1 KIA VC possible—also receiving more fire from same location—calling in Arty.

Pfc Mike Thibault, 3rd Plt-Oregon City, OR Forward Observer:

The artillery was called for but denied, as they said it was Danger Close to our troops. Unfortunate call—we could have adjusted. The artillery was straight forward and in total unfortunate. I asked for coordinates and they fired about three rounds. It was about 100 yards or more off. It turns out it may well have been between our lines and the VC leadership. But, Charlie, the enemy, was in the process of moving closer and trying to overrun us. So, I asked the artillery to drop 100 and fire for effect. Whoever was on their radio questioned me and said that might be too close. I told him that we were in the process of being overrun and repeated drop 100 and fire for effect. They wouldn't do it. Then Sgt Charlie Morris called over and asked why the artillery stopped and I told him. He told me that their radio had been shot up and to bring my radio over and he would straighten them out. I took the radio through a shit storm of fire where Sgt Morris was. He asked where my rifle was and I told him it was jammed with mud. He told me to go back, clean the rifle and put it into play. I did that going back through that shit storm of fire. The first time I was shot, I was cleaning the rifle. So that's what happened with the artillery, my radio, my rifle, and me. No one put any more artillery into play. I have no idea why."

Note, as his commander, I would be made aware of additional actions that he took that day part of which Thibault writes about in his testimony. Based on his action that I was made aware of, I recommended him for the Bronze Star Medal for Valor.

Duty Officer's Log 1137 - A Co getting hit bad--No clearance for Arty (Reply) Clearance obtained. --Arty now on the way.

Artillery finally being approved, our Forward Observer Lt. Frank Pascerella and his Radio Telephone Operator (RTO) of the 3d Bn, 319th Arty, began placing artillery to the rear and west of the 3rd Plt to block the enemy falling back or reinforcing their move against the 3rd Plt.

(Pascarella was the epitome of professionalism and teamwork. He would be killed in action during his second tour in Vietnam.)

Photo of "Doc" Beaton- Sr, Medic for Co A, and Lt Passarella Arty FO

The Artillery unit that was in direct support of our company was A Battery, 3d Bn of the 319th Field Artillery (Airborne) with their 105mm Artillery M1 cannons. Their support would provide us with artillery out to a range of o/a

52

11,000 meters. Additionally, we were able to select specific types of artillery rounds (based on our needs that time) but mainly the High Explosive rounds (HE). Captain Hugh Socks was the Battery Commander and was a "gold dust" asset to us on June 29th and elsewhere.

As observed by Capt. Harold Brent, Artillery Officer: "One of the things we learned was that accurate artillery fire was depended not only on the artillery battery supporting us but the forward observers. Lt Pascarella, our main guy, was the chief, but in each of the three rifle platoons there was a forward observer that came out of our weapons platoon. This team was critical when we got in trouble.

Indirect artillery fire required three components working in concert to deliver the 105mm rounds on to the enemy. Accurate fire began with an observer, as we just mentioned, radioing the battery Fire Direction Center (FDC) requesting the 105mm shells at a specific location or from a concentration point. That we had previously had fired in. The battery FDC computed the settings necessary for the guns to deliver them those settings were telephoned from the FDC to the guns. The gun crews used the settings to prepare a specific artillery shell, shoved it into the gun, set guns to the correct bearing and…fired when ordered. Those settings from the FDC included the type of shell, the proper fuse and time settings.

The guns were called to fire and given the computed settings from the FDC. Game ON. In most cases gun number three (Base piece) shot to register on the requested location, five other guns copied base piece settings, and all six guns fired rounds. This was a great moment!

Rule number one for combat by our company…Never get outside of A Battery's artillery range!"

Duty Officer's Log 1140 - A Co reports getting hit bad, mortar-50 cal MG-small arms. Using all Arty available. Looks like a base camp.

Duty Officer's Log 1145 - Bn req from Bde light fire team--have them come up in 2/503 net.

Duty Officer's Log 1146 - Bde to Bn- LFT is abn now, will come upon 2/503 net.

Duty Officer's Log 1147 - Bn req Bde to have airstrike on alert- Not Not to scramble anyone yet.

Duty Officer's Log 1154 - Bde to Bn Air controller will be over area shortly.

Duty Officer's Log 1155 - Bn to Bde-A/2 getting hit hard with 50 cal machine guns, mortars, an small arms. Using all arty available looks like base camp may need air alert ALO. Do not scramble aircraft.

Duty Officer's Log 1155 - A Co 1st Platoon receiving reinforcement from A Co - 3d Plt stationary and pretty well chewed up.

By this time the 3d Platoon had been in contact for an hour and a half and the other three platoons are nearing their position. The VC were in two fortified positions consisting of bunkers, entrenchments and upwards to 80 auto and crew served weapons. One interesting note is that this position had been designated by the Bn S2 in the Operations Orders as Objective Ord as a primary, priority objective and a possible enemy position. We were to check it out before moving to other objectives. We did, and it was. The Bn S-2 was right. In hindsight, it turned out to be an objection. It appears now that the enemy force was pulling back.

(Note for a description of the actions by the 3rd Platoon up until this point see the following):

The following is the Official Report by Capt John Coker of the S2 Office 173d Abn Bde. Interview of 3rd Platoon WIA in 3d MASH and 93d EVAC by Capt Coker, 2/503. June 30, 1966 (the next day) indicated the following:

1. Enemy

It seems there were two different types of VC engaged at the location. Several people saw (a) green or tiger striped fatigue uniforms, steel helmets, and web gear, others (b) saw black pajamas, white headbands, no helmets or web gear, and still others saw both.

2. Contact

(a) Initially, contact started when the point squad (Morris) went to check out what looked like a bunker, but turned out to be a large latrine, (several people stated that the area was covered with latrines and slit trenches (think: large force) and it was evident that dysentery was common (note in another AA report it was pointed out that the 308th had a malaria problem). The first VC sighted wore black pajamas, white headband and no weapons. The lead squad fired on these people, knocking down three or four, then the 50 cal machine gun fired on the point squad, forcing them to withdraw. The first few minutes of the fight was characterized by machine gun fire, both 50 cal and 30 cal, but very little small arms fire. Later (approximately 20 min) the platoon was hit from three sides and then the fourth side with heavy fire from small arms, rifle grenades, and hand grenades, M-79, recoilless rifle, 50 cal, 30 cal and mortar. One NCO stated he saw a tree approximately 8 inch in diameter, cut down six to eight feet above the ground by what he thought was a direct fire weapons, probably a recoilless rifle. The machine gun fire came from elevated positions, some people believed from trees. One machinegun (50 cal) was behind the platoon, firing on them. Two 30 cal machineguns had interlocking fire.

55

Almost everyone talked about hearing the VC NCO's and officers shouting and yelling. One man stated that he knew a little Vietnamese and he heard someone calling "come here". Another stated that one VC shouted in English "Surrender, we kill all of you" however no one else remembered hearing this.

All of the NCO's interviewed stated that the VC maneuvered with a high degree of professionalism. The VC concentrated their fire on the people who were talking or shouting directions. The VC would place semi-automatic fire on a wide front, and when they attracted returned fire, would concentrate on the spot with machine guns.

Most of the grenades used were black, shaped like a smoke grenade, with no wooden handle. Many of these were duds. The VC threw grenades during the entire fight.

The twelve people interviewed stated they saw a total of 32 VC go down when hit.

One person stated he saw the brass from a 3.5 rocket launcher, but was vague on describing it.

Personnel also complained about the canister rounds for the M-79. They said the 12-gauge shotgun worked fine, but the canister rounds were duds.

Duty Officer's Log 1156 - Light Fire Team (LFT) returning to Xuan Loc to rearm.

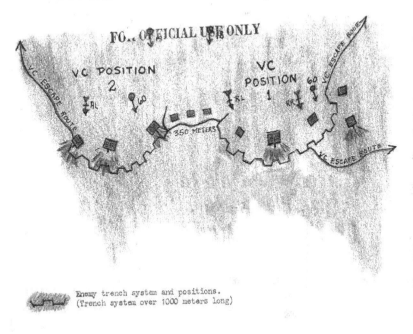

Enemy trench system and positions.
(Trench system over 1000 meters long)

Pfc Bill Palmer 3d Plt from Dayton, Ohio:

I remember the barrel of the M60 machine gun glowing red and the difficult time we had changing barrels. It was also about this time that a burst of gunfire hit between me and I believe Simmons on my right, and from the angle the tracer rounds came it was obviously to our rear and high like it came from in the trees. As I turned and probably came up to more of a sitting position to look up I was immediately hit in the back probably from a position directly in front of us. While I

57

remained in control, I was stunned by the impact and I knew I was in trouble because every time I took a breath the air was escaping from the opening in my back and just making a gurgling sound. My life was probably saved by someone near me that managed to find a large piece of plastic wrapping and tightly secured that over the opening in my back making it easier to breath. I later learned that I was hit twice by (probably) a 30 caliber machine gun; both bullets had punctured my right lung and both hit ribs fracturing them but keeping the bullets from exiting which doctors felt contributed to my survival. One thing I have always been amazed at was the discipline of the platoon in maintaining composure and continuing to fight despite knowing we would probably be overrun; thankfully they were never able to. Later I was lifted out by an Air Force Rescue helicopter that winched me up into it.

Duty Officer's Log 1214 - Bn to Bde LFT has not come up on the net at this time.

By this time the 1st Platoon is attacking the Position #1 in the North and 2nd Platoon and Weapons are attacking Position #2 in the South. (Also see copies of additional witness statements. These are 14 witness reports by members of the 1st, 2nd and 3rd Platoons.)

Duty Officer's Log 1216 - Bn req Forward Air Controller orbit E of 58- N of 04-Arty about to fire.

Duty Officer's Log 1247 - A Co reports estimate of from 75 to 100 VC. 1st element (1st Platoon) about to close on the 3rd Plt - (Position #2) 1st (Platoon) element about 150 meters away from 3rd Platoon.

One of the untold stories of this battle and all battles of the Vietnam War was the heroism and conduct of the combat medics that were in the infantry units. That was certainly the case in A Company. Our medics were: Doc Robert Beaton the senior medic, was in headquarters section, Sgt Lee Short in the 1st Platoon, an unknown medic in the 2nd Platoon, Malcolm Berry in the 3rd Platoon and Rice in the Weapons Platoon.

(Sgt Morris would share his appreciation of Sp Malcolm Berry, his platoon medic in these words: "I saw Berry leave his position and go to the aid of a wounded soldier. He totally disregarded the incoming fire to assist the man to a position that offered some cover where he could be treated. He later again left his position under heavy fire and came to assist me and another wounded man. I was bleeding from a chest wound and he told me to stay down…and even sat on me to try and keep me down. Eventually he left to assist other wounded under a hail of enemy fire and incoming grenades. He was hit again. His example was an inspiration to all who saw him. Sp Malcom Berry would be awarded the Silver Star, for gallantry in action posthumously.")

Duty Officer's Log 1310 - Lead element 3d Platoon A Co not under fire now. 3rd Platoon has reports he came under heavy fire from the West of his original position. Other elements are within 100 meters of his position.

Pfc Mike Sturges, 3d Plt:

We were the last squad of the 3rd Plt. We had encountered a few shots during the move, then silence, and then a few more-and then all hell broke loose. We were taking fire from all directions. There was a MG off to the right – a 50 cal raking us. I had the M-79 guy put rounds on it and it seemed to stop. Where we were there was no real cover. Shasteen and I noticed some trees forward and crawled towards them—encountered trenches and a bunker—then came under heavy fire and had to pull back. There were lots of wounded including Sgts Fritts and Hido—I worked on them. The fire picked up and we had machine guns, rocket propelled grenades, mortars and grenades coming at us and what seemed like a big orange football—not sure what that was. I was spending time pulling bodies back to a mound where there were already a lot of bodies. We were just about out of ammo, I recall redistributing ammo and taking dressings off the dead to use on the live wounded as we were out of dressings. I recall patching up Sgt Morris, the RTO was killed, but I heard someone around the radio saying "if they hit us once more we're all dead". We formed a small perimeter, and discussed what we'd do if we were about to be captured. Then I saw a GI helmet coming towards us—it was Woody Davis of the 1ˢᵗ Platoon.

(Sturges would receive the Bronze Star for Valor for his actions.)

Sgt Charles B. Morris, 3d Plt, Carroll County, VA, (Medal of Honor Recipient):

As the relief force entered our area, Chaplain Connie Walker was the first man to reach me. I was in tears; I had lost some of the best fighting men in the world. Many of my boys, I knew, would never fight for their country again. I tried to show the chaplain the most severely wounded, but he realized our state of mind and immediately had prayer with me, then went to every man. While praying with PFC William Marshall of Detroit, he noticed that the young soldier was bleeding heavily above the tourniquet on his arm, which had been blown off below the elbow. Chaplain Walker used part of his own clothing and quickly applied another tourniquet high on the arm and stopped the bleeding.

After rendering spiritual aid, the chaplain started chopping trees to try and clear an LZ for the evacuation of the wounded and dead. I've never seen a man in my life work as hard as he did. The chaplain is a 'mighty big man'. He seemed to be a tower of strength. Every time that my vision cleared so that I could see, I saw him working like a buzz saw. He even held huge trees as they were being chopped down, using a 'bear hug' and moved them to avoid hitting our wounded comrades. I could never express the respect and appreciation Chaplain Walker won that bloody day.

(Chaplain Walker would receive the Silver Star medal for this and other actions on that day.)

Duty Officer's Log 1312 - A Co (3d Platoon) now receiving hand grenades and MG fire from West...still surrounded.

Lt. Vose, Plt Ldr 1st Plt, Miami, FL:

I heard the Company Commander talking to SSgt Cooney 3rd Plt Ldr, and I got Cooney on the radio and said we were close and expect us soon . . . we then encountered 12.7 machine gun, we dropped packs, I left 1 man to guard them and put platoon online with 2 M60

61

machine guns in the center and we massed fire and it ended the enemy firing.

Pfc Bubber Fishburne, 1st Plt, Manchester, GA:

There were three men ahead of me as we approached the firefight. John Bertel, the Fire Team Leader, and the second man in our squad, was killed instantly as a 30 ca. machine gun round hit his cheek and went down into his chest. Sgt Showalter also caught a around which ruined his shoulder, and Tibbs was hit in the forehead. Our platoon medic Jones was right there to tend to him. The jungle was so thick that we didn't bother to search for enemy dead. Soon we reached the 3rd Plt and the sight was indescribable. I won't even try. If I could describe it like I saw it, you'd be as sick as I was.

Duty Officer's Log 1322 - Bn to Bde- No confirmation on 3d Platoon being surrounded-waiting for further details.

(It's at this time that the 2d Plt, the Wpns Plt and Command Group have closed and are moving through Position #2 and into Position #1 to join with the 1st Plt.)

1st Lt. Vendetti, Wpns Plt, Townline, NY:

All units were to help 3rd platoon because it was taking heavy fire. Weapons Plt, which was with 2nd platoon, had just come upon a VC Position which was about 8 foot higher than the surrounding area where there was a 50 Cal and 2- 30 Cal machine guns set up. The 50 and one 30 cal was abandoned but the other 30 cal was *firing at 3rd platoons position. We started taking on fire ourselves and moved off the hill where guns were set up to obtain some cover. I then radioed the 1st platoon leader, Bill Vose and told him where the firing was coming from and 1st platoon took the 30 cal out, his platoon ended the heavy fire. The VC were bugging out. Weapons continued toward 3rd platoon's position. The jungle was thick and I noticed that the VC had cut channels in the foliage to obtain a better advantage of getting eyes on the enemy. As we approached 3rd platoon's we came upon many wounded and dead. It was a horrible scene. The area smelled again of, urine, gunpowder, smoke, and now blood. Body parts were all over. Very few of the dead were VC. The sights and sounds I will never forget.*

Simmons and Shasteen - 3rd Plt

63

Card and Turner - Weapons Plt

Duty Officer's Log 1330 - Bn to Bde- A Co still engaged; no further details no.

Duty Officer's Log 1445 - (Late entry)- A Co report they have suffered some causalities will secure position in 10 minutes, have knocked out three bunkers - Arty laid on to block VC retreat.

Duty Officer's Log 1530 - (Late Entry) A Co secured area believed 100 VC opposing his elements. Has determined 1 dead, 4 walking wounded m his elements. Does not know at this time how many VC have been wounded or killed.

After the battle had died down we were trying to get our wounded out, and enemy small arms fire continued to delay the extraction of wounded. When all seemed to be at a standstill, our Chaplain, Connie Walker, moved past me and said, *"It's O.K. Captain, I'll get them out."* He moved to a small cleared area where we were trying to get dust offs and other helicopters to lower cables so that we could wench out or just pull up the wounded (triple canopy of trees) and get them to a MASH (Mobile Army Surgical Hospital). It seemed to me that each time a helicopter was near, we'd pick up incoming fire. The Chaplain would say, *"It's OK, bring him here to me,"* and then he would tie the soldier onto the rope or harness, and out the wounded would go. Walker would receive the Silver Star Medal for gallantry in action for his actions that day. He was our *"Shepard in the valley of death"* and stood in the gap for us. (See more on Chaplain Walker in his book: ***The Leapin' Deacon - The Soldier's Chaplain***, Lang Marc Publishing, Austin, Texas 2004.)

Chaplain Walker

Pfc Jack Milner, 3d Plt, Decatur, GA:

Sgt Morris' words picked up the morale of the platoon. After the fight went on for a while many of the men got hit. Sergeant Morris started taking care of them. I looked at him taking care of another fellow and he had blood running from every part of his body. Sergeant Morris never stopped for a moment. He crawled to most all of the positions checking the men. When he was not taking care of the men he was talking on the radio. When he was not talking on the radio he was fighting at the front and keeping the Viet Cong from charging our line. To sum it all up, 1) He was our platoon leader when Sergeant Cooney got hit, 2) He was our medic when the medic got killed, 3) He was our RTO when the RTO got hit, and 4) He was the greatest squad leader I ever saw.

Duty Officer's Log 1540 - A Co reports blood trails leading from VC positions. Found rice, 1 -30 cal MG, shovels and misc items.

Duty Officer's Log 1600 - A Co reports 17 walking wounded, 2 KIA (Friendly). No count on VC. At this time no bodies. Also found all types of pers gear (enemy).

Duty Officer's Log 1630 - A Co requests dust-off be sent to this area at this time. Dust off over this position now does not have proper equipment.

Duty Officer's Log 1720 (?) - A Co reports 35 wounded, 10 KIA (friendly) - Dust-off now in A Co loc dropping off morphine

Duty Officer's Log 1623 - Bde requisitioning more info from A Co.

Duty Officer's Log 1635 - Bde req loc for A Co

Duty Officer's Log 1724 - Bn rept to Bde- A Co 45 casualties, 35 WIA 10 KIA- VC loses unknown.

2d Platoon took over the VC positions

Duty Officer's Log 1810 - A Co rpts that 1 VC WIA has expired Total VC casualties are 1 VC KIA(BC) and 21 KIA(est) Also heard many bodies being dragged away.

Duty Officer's Log 1830 - A Co reports all but 16 casualties have been evac

Duty Officer's Log 1841- A Co reports have 6 WIA to be evacuated and 10 KIA.

Stuff does happen, and after one particular Dust-Off the crew of that helicopter would experience a memorable event. When we finally got Sgt Morris loaded into the Dust Off we had placed him in a body bag along with a number of captured enemy documents (these documents would be used to prevent the VC attack on the ARVN compound at Xa Gia Ray as reported by Capt. Boykin Bn S-2). Here's the "memorable event":

Morris was lifted out in a body bag from a very tight Pick Up zone where the Dust Off couldn't land, and therefore he (the body bag) was attached to a rope and yanked out so the Dust Off could clear the surrounding trees. We were informed that the Dust Off en route to the MASH had to land and move Morris/body bag inside the aircraft to continue the flight. When the Dust Off crew got out of the chopper to move the body bag inside he aircraft for the remainder of the flight they saw the body bag begin to move and shake. When they unzipped it- there was Morris. He was not dead, but alive! For the crew it was a "Come to Jesus" moment. "Stuff", does also end well!

> **Duty Officer's Log 1855** - Huskies with less seriously WIA from A Co are landing at Bn loc.
> **Duty Officer's Log 1900** - A Co CP loc at 573013, another element as 581001.
> **Duty Officer's Log 1915 - A Co plans to consolidate at the LZ on which casualties are left.**

Once the company was organized into a defensive position for the night, measures were accomplished to defend if we were attacked. This was a standard operating procedure that we always employed and included: ensuring we had interlocking fires with our machine guns, claymore mines, and mortar and artillery defensive fires.

The machine guns would have tracer rounds fired and that would really have enhanced the coverage being maximized. The tracer round had a small pyrotechnic charge in its base. The charge ignited by the burning powder burns brightly making the projectile trajectory visible to the naked eye during day or night time. This enables the gunner to make aiming corrections without observing the impact of the rounds and without sights of the weapon. Tracers are usually loaded as every fifth round in machine gun belts.

(The M18A1 Claymore mine was a directional, anti-personnel mine used by us for ambushed and defensive positions. It was command detonated and shot a pattern of metal balls into a kill zone like a shotgun out to about 110 yards within a 60-degree arch.)

Listening Posts were established out in front of each platoon. This would normally be a two-man element located o/a 25 to 50 meters out in front of their platoon. The Artillery Forward Observer, Lt Passarella, would have the artillery, (Battery A of the $3^{rd}/319^{th)}$ fire in defensive concentrations so that if we needed artillery support we already had known concentration points that we could fire at or fire from when needed. Once all of that was done we were ready for the night with at least one person in each foxhole alert at all times.

Artillery was a significant "battle field optimizer" that we had and it came from A Battery, 3rd Battalion 319th Airborne Artillery. Capt Hugh Socks was the battery commander and was always ready to support us when called on.

Duty Officer's Log 2045 - CO 2d Bn to CO A Co: Essence of conversation concerning status of morale,

69

personnel, equipment and causalities and CO A Co plans for tomorrow. Casualty count was reconfirmed, A Co will return to area where bunkers and supplies were loc. Resupply was received. 3rd Platoon is badly decimated; the unit morale is excellent.

Duty Officer's Log 2150 - Two Huskies at A Co loc first light.

Duty Officer's Log 2150 - No contact with A Co.

Duty Officer's Log 2299 - We have contact with A Co thru aerial relay.

Duty Officer's Log 2205 - A Co was advised of Huskies at his location at 1st light, to extract his KIA, US weapons, any enemy materials of intel value and misc. cargo.

Duty Officer's Log 2230 - Bde: Huskie that was req will be in area at 0700 instead of 1st light. A Co notified.

Duty Officer's Log 2235 - A Co continues with planned operation for tomorrow but be careful. Area will probably be bobby trapped.

Duty Officer's Log 2245 - Huskie for tomorrow has been cancelled. Job will be done with a CH-47 at the same time

"Stand To – The Company is alerted to prepare for night defensive positions. Artillery night defensive targets were fired in and noted for future artillery fire requests and adjustments. Communications checked. Claymores are positions and Listening Posts are set out.

It has been a tough day and now it seems, hopefully, a time for rest yet still on alert. Thoughts are many—KIA and WIA reported and visually remembered each face. Resupply was delivered but there needs to be more before we move out in the

morning. All seems quiet, but it also seems that we might be mortared or attacked at any time. I'm sure that in each foxhole there is a different mix of feeling and thoughts, Who got hit? What did each of us do or not do? Thoughts of back home, thoughts of songs - "Paula," "Ticket to Ride," "Yesterday," and "When A Man Loves A Woman". Thoughts of hours left until morning and stand to. What will tomorrow be like? What will we face then...hopefully not a repeat of today. Just maybe it's a time in preparation for tomorrow—it's a time for prayers. Dear Lord, be with us through this night and in our movement tomorrow; place a hedge of angels around us and bless and keep us in Your hands."

Viet Cong bunkers captured by Co A

71

2nd Battalion Summary

The 2nd Bn (Abn), 503rd Inf retained its perimeter defense posture during the first seven hours of this reporting period. The CP remains in the same location. Ambush sites and LP's were established during the hours of darkness the morning of 29 June with negative results. At 0200 hours of the Recon Plt conducted patrol activities at and around cord 502019 returning with neg information. At 0700 implementation of Frag Order # 3 began. This order required Co's A, B and C to conduct helicopter assaults on LZ's Brazil, Chile and Peru, respectively saturate these AO's with squad size patrols select and prepare an extraction LZ and be prepared for extraction o/a 1 July. The initial assault by A Co was unopposed as was B & C Co's assault. A continuous airstream of 30 HU1D helicopters in increments of 10 each lift was required to deploy the companies. The following situations developed as a result of the units patrolling actions; at coordinates 596004, Co A discovered 16 prone type foxholes oriented to the SE that appeared to be 3-4 days old. At 1035 hours Co A's 3rd Plt encountered an enemy force at coordinates 580993. In the ensuing battle it developed that the platoon has engaged approximately 75-100 VC that were in fortified positions consisting of bunkers, entrenchments and upwards to 80 auto and crew served weapons. It was immediately apparent that the platoon was outnumbered and they called upon the Company to provide enforcement. In the meantime the platoon came under fire from the North, South, and West from automatic weapons and mortar, which began to inflict heavy casualties. The supporting artillery provided all available fire for the beleaguered platoon, which relieved the situation for somewhat. Reinforcements at 1155 hours and began deploying against the enemy position. This action, plus

72

the supporting fire, caused the enemy force to break contact and the position was overrun and secure at 1215 hours. Review journal entry 66-130 for detailed entries on engagement. Total casualties inflicted on US forces numbered 10 KIA and 35 WIAs. Total VC 1KIA (BC).

JOURNAL CLOSED 292400H Jun 66 MSG SULLIVAN

Note: Reports from Lessons Learned that were forwarded to the USA Army Pacific Command noted that A Company had engaged the 308th VC Main Force Battalion, part of the 274th VC Regiment in a base camp with an estimated 150 VC. Additional Aviation reports that Brigade aircraft were fired on by the enemy 16 separate times sustaining one hit.

In Reflection—It finally became night!We thought all was secure but were extra alert for an enemy attack. I feel sure that many of the troopers were storing up memories never to be forgotten. For me it was specifically that—capturing each important event that had occurred and never forgetting. Most of all, the words of Sgt Morris spoken just before he was evacuated on a Dust-Off helicopter, "Sir, leave me for last, don't leave anyone else behind." Over the past fifty-two years I will remember them always. I now use them in talks, speeches, and sermons. Not only is it our responsibility to seek out those that are in trouble, in need, or lost, and then offer them help; especially to those facing a spiritual battle. In Isaiah 6:8 are the words from the Lord, "whom shall I send and who will go for us? Here am I send me." It's a call on my life to offer Christ to anyone that has yet to accept Him as Savior, and for them to receive eternal life!

The following day—June 30th

We made it through the night.(check Bn Log for enemy activity) Now it's time to move again, and this time to join up again with the Battalion. During our time in our defensive position following our battle, the Company XO, Captain Southerd was back in Bien Hoa having our resupply requests filled and made ready for the re-supply helicopters to lift them to us. First, there were casualties to lift out—and ammo was critically low. There was the need for resupply of that ammunition that we had expended the previous day. Then based on the following mission, additional supplies were requested. The missions could change and we could not afford to be caught short on something needed and not asked for.

Our battle location as well as back at Bien Hoa, were both busy times. One important and critical administrative responsibility was to get those letters to next of kin of our men who had been killed in action. As soon as our reports were sent back to our base at Bien Hoa, then further notification of those KIA was sent through Department of Army to those hometowns where our soldiers were from. There through a military procedure, Survivor Assistance Officers SAO), would be appointed and immediately be sent to notify the parents or next of kin of those KIA. They would provide as much information as available regarding the circumstances of the member's death and answer any questions. The SAO would also ensure that the survivors' immediate needs were being met during this difficult time.

Having served in that capacity myself, I know it is a time of sorrow and pain as the notifications were made; when the residence is approached and the door opens, the message is read and it becomes a heartrending time of disbelief, sorrow, and pain.

My wife, Lynn, would share from her experience about one day when she looked out from our home in Augusta, GA and saw an Army sedan driving up and down the street in front of her home. Ft. Gordon was located there and had a large population of military families. Finally, the driver stopped and approached our house. Her feeling was of shock and fear that I had been killed. Finally, the army officer knocked on the door and when she opened it he apologized and said he was a Survivor Assistance Officer (SAO). He was looking for an address in our neighborhood but couldn't find it. He was inquiring with her to see if she would know where he could find it. It could have been me, as well as one of the 58,195 of our soldiers, sailors, airmen and marines who were killed during that conflict.

Back to that day in June of 1966 we are not sure what the new day will hold for us, other than patrolling around our defensive area to insure we have policed up any enemy bodies, weapons, or other items of intelligence value. Then on, or about 11:30, we began to prepare for the move to our next location.

There are two things that are on our mind; first to insure that we are combat ready to move out. That all the leaders are briefed on the who, what, where, and how we are moving. No time to be slack as we are certain that we have met a large enemy force, and they are perhaps still in our area on the route we will be taking. Then, who was the enemy force that we met?

June 30, 1966 Daily Staff Journal or Duty Officer's Log- 2/503 Inf -Vic Xuan Loc

> **Duty Officer's Log 0035** - Neg contact with Bn
> **Duty Officer's Log 0100** - Contact with Bn thru arty net
> **Duty Officer's Log 0115** - Contact with Bn

Duty Officer's Log 0145 - Commo with Bn
Duty Officer's Log 0445 - Commo with Bn thru relay
Duty Officer's Log 0530 - Company went to Stand To

"Stand To," is a military procedure dating back to previous wars. For us it was a half hour time period where all troops were to be alert, checking weapons and commo gear - lasting o/a 30 minutes usually just at twilight and also at first light in the morning. Having completed stand to earlier, it was now the right time for the First Sergeant and I to walk the perimeter. We still had 3 KIA's to be evacuated and the extraction was laid on. As we walked the positions we were checking to insure that they were dug in in anticipation of a counterattack by the VC, and also to insure that the recon patrols had been sent out. As we moved around our perimeter, checking out the positions, we stopped to talk to the 13 men left in the 3rd platoon. I told them they had done a great job and, tried to share their grief. I then told them that since there were only 13 left, I planned to have them become part of one of the other two platoons. At that time PFC Freeman Oates stepped up to me, just about nose to nose, and said... *"Captain, there's only 13 of us, and we are all PFC's, but I'm the ranking PFC and we don't need to be put in other platoons. We're still a platoon and we need to stay that way."*

That sounded good to me and I told Lt. Vendetti, who was the Weapons Platoon Leader, to take over the 3rd Platoon and take SSgt Willie Pitts, who was with the Weapons Platoon, to be the 3rd Platoon Sergeant—along with the help of PFC Oates. MSgt Louis Pigeon took over as the Weapons Platoon Leader.

(As a note: PFC Oates would be later recognized by being awarded the Bronze Star with Valor award for his actions on this day.)

Duty Officer's Log 0725 - Fm A Co- documents captured indicate units are D-3 Bn (308th VC MF Bn) and C-11 Company. Cartridges found are: 75 mm, 57mm, 50 cal and Chi Com grenades.

Duty Officer's Log 0730 - A Co evacuating KIA, intel documents, US weapons and other misc. cargo.

Duty Officer's Log 0750 - A Co requesting two chain saws and a long rope. Also requesting that the helo who carried out the chainsaws bring back bag of documents and the 1 KIA.

LZ Torres

The LZ that we cleared was a miracle. We had chainsaws and explosives, but soon had to ask for a resupply of

77

more chainsaws and explosives. Our 1st Sgt, Tony Torres, took on the responsibility to insure that it got cleared. Tough job! He did it well and we called it "LZ Torres". (Two thoughts on 1st Sgt Torres,(a) throughout our time together in Co A whenever we experienced one of our guys being KIA, and the Dust Off was coming, he'd grab me and say, "Sir, we need to carry our guy to the Dust Off", and (b) shortly after this battle, Torres would be promoted to Command Sergeant Major and become the CSM of the 4th Battalion—a professional and one great soldier.)

> **Duty Officer's Log 0800** - A Co has only evacuated the WIA, KIA's not evac as of yet. Also A Co received only one Chinook chopper w/ hand winch.
> **Duty Officer's Log 0852** - A Co found 13 green uniforms (brand new) that look like our aggressor uniforms.
> **Duty Officer's Log 0912** - Helicopter on the way to Bde with documents and 1 KIA.
> **Duty Officer's Log 0921** - A Co chain saw arr. 4 KIA out.

What was left of 3rd Platoon

Resupply - I felt it important to place the issue of resupply somewhere in the text. So I am asking you to consider the following when we discuss resupply. Once the initial fight has subsided the immediate concern is for resupply of ammunition and other need supplies as well as the treatment of casualties. Although we see the rapid response in the medical areas if we are to continue the fight there are other needs as well such as:

C-Rations - Ever consider what the troops were eating in the field? Basically, it came down to "C Rations" These items of canned meals came in a box with a several choices: Ham and eggs chopped-B-3; Pork steak B-3; Beef sliced with sauce B-3; Chicken Boned B-3A; Ham and lima beans B-3; Meatballs with Beans and Tomatoes Sauce B-2; Beef Slices with Potatoes with Gravy B-2; Beans and Frankfurters Chunks with Tomato Sauce

B-2; Turkey Loaf B-1A; Ham Fried B-1A; Beef Steak B-1A; Chicken and Noodles B1A. The key here is that if there was an A after the item it meant there was a fruit can in the packet. It could be peaches, pears or fruit cocktail., The fruit packets were the most sought after - and the First Sergeant would often turn the box over so that a trooper wouldn't know what he was selecting- and this would prevent all the fruit being taken by the first in line-It was a gourmet feast! .

A-Rations - this meant that we would have hot food being in stored in marmite cans, where the company would file by and fill their mess kits out of the marmite cans, an insulated food container with 8 inserts that hot or cold food could also carry 24-12 oz cans. A-Rations were impossible...it takes too long and a very dangerous undertaking if contact is imminent. Needless to say, we didn't have A-Rations on Operations Yorktown.

> **Duty Officer's Log 0925** - A Co requested one basic load of explosives.
> **Duty Officer's Log 0931** - A Co 3 bodies left to extract.

Pfc Mack Dennard facing General Westmoreland with Pfc William Carrier behind.

Duty Officer's Log 1050 - A Co while sweeping area where contact was made found black uniforms, civilian uniforms, 15 or more brand new hammocks, sweaters & jackets also 800 lbs of rice and dried fish.

Duty Officer's Log 1112 - A Co has completed extraction and will be moving to next objective, which will take 20 minutes. Req C4 explosive to prepare LZ, which will take 20 min. Req C4 explosive to prepare LZ, which will take 3-4 hours.

Duty Officer's Log 1116 - C4 enroute to A Co loc, 585016.

Duty Officer's Log 1150 - Co A located at 586007 heard noises to their south and are checking it out now.

Duty Officer's Log 1204 - Bn commo check.

Duty Officer's Log 1215 - Fm Bde - documents indicate that A Co ran into contact with en one Bn from the 274th Regt.

Pfc Warren Weissenbacher, Rifleman, 3rd Plt - Niles, CA:

Five of us new guys were replacements for 3rd Plt on June 30th. It was quite an introduction to A Co. Our first day joining A co. at the base camp in Bien Hoa we were told to report to the 3rd Plt area - when we got there a Sgt took us to the 3rd Plt area- old large canvas tents- and he said to throw our duffel bags into one of the tents and a chopper would be by soon to take us out to where the 3rd Plt was. We were in our nice new jungle fatigues and had no other gear. The Sgt said don't worry about it- you'll get some. Less than an hour later the chopper arrived and flew us way out into some jungle area- dropped us off and a Sgt came out of the jungle and said to follow him. He took us to a large pile of rucksacks, pistol belts, M-16's, canteens, helmets and said to pick out the equipment we needed. Some of the stuff was messed up, damaged, we noticed bullet holes and some dried blood and we realized this gear was from the 3rd Plt firefight the day before. No personal items were in this gear. So now our pucker factor was way up there! After we suited up and went into the 3rd Plt area, some of the guys all pretty dirty and rough looking, looked at us new guys in our clean jungle fatigues and wearing their buddies' gear—they just kind of rolled their eyes at us.

Duty Officer's Log 1217 - A Co was moving but heard rifle butts closing and also heard people so they stopped to check the area out

Duty Officer's Log 1240 - CO 2d Bn for A Co use Arty in area where they heard noise before going on.

Duty Officer's Log 1300 - A Co moving

Duty Officer's Log 1400 - A Co discovered on 29 June numerous enemy foxholes seemingly two to three weeks old at Coord 600006.

Duty Officer's Log 1425 - Bn to A Co upon reaching planned position. Search paths of VC withdrawal for poss VC bodies.

The following was received from Captain Boykin, our Battalion S-2:

"On June 29, 1966, near Xuan Loc, Republic of Vietnam, Company A, 2d Battalion (Airborne) 503d Infantry, seized the Battalion Headquarters of the 308th Main Force Battalion (Viet Cong) after a furious battle. A number of documents were captured by Company A, including an operations plan for the attack on the Army of Vietnam garrison at Xa Gia Ray and the subsequent ambush of the relief column coming from Xa Xuan Loc. When the garrison at Xa Gia Ray came under attack the relief column, now aware of the Viet Cong trap, preceded their movement with an airstrike in the area where the ambush was expected. Upon arrival in the area, they found over 20 dead Viet Cong and the main force had fled. Foreknowledge of the Viet Cong plan prevented the destruction of the relief column and enabled it to reinforce the beleaguered garrison at Xa Gia Ray. The Viet Cong broke contact at Xa Guia Ray

and withdrew. Among the other documents captured by Company A was a dairy which described the high rate of malaria in the 308th Main Force Battalion (Viet Cong) and identified other enemy units in the area. A sheet of the current Viet Cong pass-words was also captured."

General Westmoreland with Ltc. Walsh, Bn Cdr – Capt Kelley, Co Cdr – SSgt Brown, Plt Ldr, 2d Plt

Duty Officer's Log 1427 - A Co presently in planned position. Will send out patrols as soon as unit dug in.

Duty Officer's Log 1815 - A Co ambush position at 578005,5778995, OP/LP at 582003,581999, 579002.

Duty Officer's Log 1817 - A Co LZ complete, ready for birds.

Duty Officer's Log 1825 - A Co LZ incomplete at this time, Will need rope to extract items.

Call from Capt. Southerd, the XO in Base Camp. Discussed future operations and supply needs to include personnel and communication needs. *Southerd mentioned my suggestion of the Silver Star for Morris wasn't appropriate. Based on initial info he had from survivors, the award should be the Medal of Honor. I agreed.*

(NOTE: from then on Southerd carried the load on this award and got personnel out to several different countries where we had troops in the hospital to get witness statements. The award of the medal to Morris was due to the actions of Capt. Ralph Southerd.)

> **Duty Officer's Log 1830** - A Co is requesting info about patrol, moving or extraction tomorrow - Bn will let you know later.
> **Duty Officer's Log 1835** - A Co resupply complete.
> **Duty Officer's Log 1900** - A Co Disregard 50 cal will stay lie we are.
> **Duty Officer's Log 1925** - Commo w/Bn thru relay.
> **Duty Officer's Log 2018** - A Co request Dust-off for 3 litter cases. Tight LZ. Need winch or Huskie. Causalities believed to be from grenades or Claymore.
> **Duty Officer's Log 2027** - A Co Confirmed 2 walking and 2 liter causalities. Wounded was from ambush loc believed to be grenades or claymore.
> **Duty Officer's Log 2130** - Huskie in A Co with/lft-in contact with A Co

The four WIA' were from the 1st Platoon. One was Pfc David Ferraro, a litter case who died a few hours after arriving at the hospital. Three WIAs were Dennis Burnett, John Price and Charles Jenkins.

Duty Officer's Log 2154 - Dust-off complete fm A Co
Duty Officer's Log 2203 - A Co rept wps not evac with
wounded- used 2 Huskies

Sgt Jim Healy, 3rd Plt, Augusta, Maine:

I left Vietnam either the 5th or 6th of July 1966. I did not go on the operation you guys were on in June. I was behind, in the base camp at Bien Hoa. I spent the night of June 28/29 monitoring radio traffic on the Battalion net. After a long uneventful night, I had returned to my squad tent to get some sleep. Sometime late in the morning of June 29th the Platoon Leader (I do not remember his name) came hobbling into the tent and woke me up. He had been wounded two or three days earlier, I think by a claymore mine, and was obviously in great distress, both physical and mental. He woke me and told me that the third platoon had hit some heavy shit and was getting shot to hell. In the course of our conversation he said that he wished he was with the platoon. He wanted to help. I know he felt helpless and so did I. I felt terrible for you guys, but hell, I had done my thing and I was ready to climb on that big silver bird and head home. I made these feelings clear to the Lt. and he left shortly after, I'm sure in great disgust. I spent the rest of that day trying to find out who had gotten hurt and who had not.

Thomas Shasteen was a hell of a brave guy; too brave. He had joined the platoon early in '66. He was just careless about his personal safety. On several occasions I had to talk to Shasteen about using just a

86

little judgment in exposing himself to danger. In each case his answer was the same "If you're going to get it, you're going to get it." I just couldn't get it through to him that he was young, felt invincible, and had just not been scared enough to get smart. He was wounded on June 29, 1966.

When I visited him in the hospital a day or two later, he entertained me with stories of fear, and described to me how fast you can dig a prone shelter with just your helmet and the proper motivation. Shasteen was a fine soldier. He was killed in an automobile accident in 1968.

I'm not sure exactly when it was I was told to go to the Graves Registration place in Long Binh to identify the guys who were killed on the 29th. It was probably a day or two after the fight and probably not the day before I left Vietnam. But, for years my recollection was that I went to Long Binh to identify these guys the day before I left Vietnam. I didn't even know that bodies had to be identified. I just assumed that they used dog tags or something. Anyway, whatever day it was, I got the word to take another guy with me and go down to Long Binh to identify the guys who were killed on the 29th. I have no idea who the guy was who went with me. He was a new guy, didn't really know anyone. I told him to agree with everything I said.

So, we drove or someone drove us down to Long Binh and these Graves Registration guys began bringing in and unzipping body bags. "Yes, that's Jones. Yes, that's Grave. Yes, that's Smith." It was eerie; very strange. The Graves Registration people were cool and calm; just doing their job. They pulled out body after body. In some cases we had to use ID cards and dog tags to make the identifications. "Yes, that's Berry, Yes, that's Surette. Yes, that's Potter." I'm sure it was my imagination, but I felt these Graves Registration guys were imploring me with their eyes, as if to say "Look, we are not really ghouls, this is our job. We'll bring them in. You identify them as fast as you can, then get the hell out of here and we will finish our job." "Yes, that's Bowman, Yes, that's Stevens, Yes, that's Berthel." The truth is, I don't remember how many of the guys I had to identify. I think all of them, but I don't remember.

I believe that Fritts and Hido were "Acting Jacks". Promoted either the same time I was or very shortly after, in late May or early June. Maybe it was the fact that we were "Acting Jacks", or maybe I just knew them a little better than I did the other guys, whatever the reason, I was particularly moved and troubled identifying them. "Yes, that's Hido. Yes, that's Fritts.

I had seen dead guys before, of course. I had carried them "out". And, I had helped put their bodies on helicopters. But, there was something different about this—identifying these guys at the Graves Registration place. It just didn't seem real. Just real, I mean, really, strange. I couldn't quite put my finger on it. They just didn't seem real, these dead men. Something was missing. Something just wasn't right.

I was uncomfortable with these thoughts as we drove back to Bien Hoa. Somewhere on the trip back I realized what was missing. There was no mud and blood, everything was clean, I mean, real clean. The bodies were clean, the Graves Registration guys were clean, and I was clean. No sweat, no mud, and no blood. There

88

was no noise, no gunfire, no explosions, no shouting, no prop wash; it was just real quiet. There was no fear, no passion, no chaos. Everything was cool, clean and orderly. It was unreal.

So, there we were this new guy, and me. He, just beginning his Vietnam experience and me ending mine. The FNG and the short timer. What a horrible beginning for him and what a lousy ending for me. I wonder who he was, and I wonder if he made it?

D. 2nd Battalion Summary

The 2nd Bn (ABN) 503d Inf continued search and destroy operations in its assigned sector of the Bde AO during this period. Co A remained generally NE, Co B east and C Co south of the CP. The CP location remained the same. Ambush sites and LP's were positioned during the hours of darkness the morning of 30 June but no enemy contact resulted.

(The rifle companies continued to saturate their search and destroy areas with squad and platoon sized patrols during the hours of daylight.)

At 0735 hours Co A received a UH47 helicopter to begin extraction of their KIA's, captured documents and other miscellaneous cargo resulting from yesterday's engagement. At 1112 hours the extraction was completed. During this period active patrolling was conducted by Co A and the following items were discovered: additional documents, indicating VC unit designations, casings from 57mm, 75mmRR. Chi Com grenades, 13 green uniforms, black uniforms, civilian clothing, hammocks and 800 lbs of rice and dried fish.)

Additional developments during this period were: the recon platoon while patrolling to the SE was subject to sniper fire from coordinates 513984 - fire was returned with unk results. Translation of documents confiscated by Co A indicated they had engaged elements from one battalion of the 274th Main Force Regiment. At coord 919538 Co C heard noises and fired into the area. Upon searching the location they found freshly matted grass indicating two or three hostiles had been there. No further daylight activities occurred.

(During the hours of darkness, ambush sites and LPs were positioned by the three line companies. One ambush site in Co A was the recipient of a Claymore device causing 3 WIAs at 2018 hrs. Dust-off for these was completed at 2154 hours)

No other enemy contact was made this period.
JOURNAL CLOSED 302400H June 66-MSG Sullivan

Often one can remember a specific combat event and easily say, "If it weren't for those one or two individuals, we would not have been successful." On June 29th, 1966 there were several key players on the battlefield that day. From my point of view they were: Sgt Charles Morris, Sp4 Malcom Berry of the 3rd Platoon, and the movement of Lt Vose and the 1st Platoon into the battle site to secure and drive off the enemy forces. Then SSgt Nat Brown's 2d Platoon's movement through and securing Position 2 and then onto to the final enemy position. And of course in hindsight, it was truly Pfc Clem Green (the mythical soldier of Company A) that enabled us to accomplish our mission that day. Well done, Pfc Clem Green!

Part Three
We Brothers-in-Arms

The Journal might be closed, but for most of us the thoughts of 50 years ago are still there. They will always remain as vivid memories. I'm hoping that as you reviewed each witness statement recorded above and following that you will remember also not only the battle, but each of the men that I served with, especially those that didn't make it.

When the battle ended we saw the enemy pushed from their two positions, and the reports from both the WIA's statements as well as testimonies from soldiers in the 1st and 2d Platoons account for a good number of enemy eliminated. There were 33 enemy KIA and a large number of enemy WIA. However, the cost for us was high in those two days as well, with 16 KIA and over 41 WIA's meaning that one of every three men in the company were killed or wounded that day. The 3d Platoon alone suffered 71% casualties—they were too far away for the remaining platoons to reinforce them in a timely manner.

Words like bravery, gallantry, and self-sacrifice were common when describing and remembering what took place. Yet, the words that best describe this day for me are these: "Greater love hath no man than this that a man lay down his life for his friends." (John 15:13 KJV)

Awards:

There were a number of awards presented in the following weeks after our battle on the 29th: Medal of Honor-1, Silver Star-3, Bronze Star with Valor device-10, Army Commendation Medal with Valor Device- 6 and 53 Purple Hearts.

At a Battalion awards ceremony at Camp Zinn the Battalion Commander, Ltc Walsh presented a number of the above awards. He called my name and presented me with the Bronze Star with Valor Device. Although he did not say the following, he should have: "Capt Kelley I am giving out this award not for what you did but for what Company A did."

When the ceremony was over I returned to where my company was standing at attention and called them to Present Arms. The guidon flashed up and then came down with a salute; I unpinned the medal off my fatigue jacket and pinned it on the guidon, which told my company that it was they who had earned it. In other occasions during my career I have had other awards presented dealing with having been in the wrong place, at the wrong time, but with the right guys. In that career of twenty years in the Army, the best "right guys" were Company A on June 29, 1966.

Who were these men of Company A? We were mostly young and from different backgrounds, religions, races, and creeds; but we had two things in common. We were all AIRBORNE SOLDIERS, and we were those who made up Company A, 2d Battalion, 503rd Airborne of the 173rd Airborne Brigade.

In his work, *King Henry 5th*, William Shakespeare would sum up our calling and remembrance like this:

"For He Who Today
Sheds His Blood with Me
Will Be My Brother
We Few
We Happy Few
We Band of Brothers"

Those who made the ultimate sacrifice (KIA) on June 29th are listed here:

- ❖ Sgt Albert Raymond Potter, Browns Mills, NJ
- ❖ SP4 Jesse Clarence Felder, Jersey City, NJ
- ❖ Sgt Frederick William Fritts, Beaumont, TX
- ❖ Sgt Richard Lee Hido, Painesville, OH
- ❖ SP4 Malcolm Crayton Berry, Hartford, CT
- ❖ PFC John Joseph Berthel, New York, NY
- ❖ PFC Robert Michael Bowman, Wilmington, DE
- ❖ PFC Frank Graves, Washington, DC
- ❖ PFC Leslie R. Smith, Indianapolis, IN
- ❖ PFC Paul Joseph Surette, Holbrook, MA
- ❖ PFC David Allen Ferraro, Pittsburgh, PA
- ❖ PFC Francis George Stevens, Ellsworth, ME
- ❖ PFC Tommy Roy Jones, Nashville, NC

Part Four
Telling it Like it Was—We were There

The following are actual accounts, or witness statements, by some of the troopers of Company A. These recollections were developed for the Operation Yorktown Report. As expected, each soldier listed below had his own experience to share.

1. PFC Patrick Burke - 3rd Platoon
2. PFC Woody Davis - 1st Platoon
3. PFC Frank Dukes - 1st Platoon
4. PFC Bubber Fishbourne - 1st Platoon
5. SP4 Jim Healy - 3rd Platoon
6. SP4 Bob Lucas - 2nd Platoon
7. PFC James Miskel - 3rd Platoon
8. SGT Charles Morris - 3rd Platoon
9. PFC Bill Palmer - 3rd Platoon
10. PFC Ron Sedlack - 3rd Platoon
11. PFC Mike Sturges - 3rd Platoon
12. 1st LT Gus Vendetti - Wpns Platoon
13. LT Bill Vose - 1st Platoon
14. PFC Warren Weissenbacher – 3rd Platoon

PFC Burke
RTO 3rd Platoon
Hyde Park, NY

I was the platoon leader's RTO and the first thing I remember about the battle on June 29 was when the enemy heavy machine guns began firing on our platoon, and the rounds were coming in right above our heads.

Being a Radio Telephone Operator, I was able to hear just about all that was going on. One thing for sure, the radio was filled with appeals for help.

One memorable and amazing thing I remembered was that the guy next to me was hit in the shoulder and it seemed his arm was shattered. What did he do? He just sat there smoking a cigarette.

When the enemy pulled back from contact with us they left it clean—no bodies or weapons were left where they had fought and suffered casualties.

Later, I was WIA on November 4th, 1967.

PFC Woody Davis
Rifleman
1st Platoon
Findlay, OH

This was hard to do (recalling the events of that day), but it's the best I can remember of June 29, 1966.

June 28 - As I recall 1st platoon had set up in the edge of a tree line overlooking a valley. There was a structure to our front, perhaps an old barn of sorts. My squad, along with Lt. Vose, cleared the structure before the platoon took defensive positions in the tree line.

After we had the platoon in position Sp4 Haynes and I were assigned to the LP approximately 70 to 80 yards down the hill from the tree line. Sgt. Showalter was to take his squad across the valley and set up an ambush site. Although we knew he was there, we could not visibly see the ambush from our position. It soon became night and all had been uneventful.

June 29 - In early morning just before or at dawn, I heard what sounded like a mortar firing from somewhere at the 10 o'clock direction, down the valley from my LP position. A split second later I heard the explosion at 1st platoon's position. I started firing my M-79 in the direction of the mortar sound I had heard, and Haynes was on the radio with Lt. Vose immediately.

Lt. Vose ran out to the LP and took over the radio to guide Sgt. Showalter's squad to the suspected mortar site to check the area. When it was cleared, everyone returned to the tree line to await the medevac for our losses. Sp4 Jesse Felder was KIA and Sp4 Brent Clover was WIA. I remember carrying Felder's body to the chopper in a double poncho liner because his arm slipped out from between the opening and hit my leg.

It was when that I realized the platoon was in immediate move out motion. We were rushing to board choppers to get to the third platoon who was engaged in a serious fucking firefight. The choppers couldn't get us close enough to them so we hit the ground running through thick jungle for what seemed forever. As we got closer, we dropped our rucks and took only weapons, ammo, and water to approach. We were using a shallow ravine and getting very close. We halted for a second, received our movement orders and started out of the ravine towards the sounds of the firefight. Berthel was first over the top and was hit immediately. That's when all hell broke loose in our direction. Vellozzi and Moore were on the M-60 and took a slightly elevated spot to bring "P" on them. Sgt. Showalter went to their area. I don't have any idea how long we were engaged, but it seemed as though our 60 won the moment not too long after they brought smoke. Just before we moved out to continue the engagement I heard the Sgt. Showalter had been hit badly, and our medic Lee B. Short was with him.

Soon after we were on line advancing toward third platoons position all the firing stopped, victor Charlie had had enough and had left the AO. As we got to the third platoon the first person I saw was Sturges. He looked straight into my eyes and I could see the relief, (I've never forgotten that look) it looked as though the M-60 he was carrying had run out of ammo.

We quickly spread out and took defensive positions. It was then that we very sickly realized that we were lying amongst the dead. We remained there until morning to be evacuated.

PFC Frank Dukes
Grenadier
1st Platoon
Lewistown, PA

I'm afraid I don't have a whole lot to offer. I was in first squad, first Platoon. Sgt. Joe Pomeroy was my squad leader. I carried an M-79 during my time in Vietnam. I do not recall our platoon being mortared at anytime. I recall getting off the choppers and securing the LZ. The next thing I remember is moving to the assembly area and then moving out. I remember that it was my day to be on the right flank of the squad. I am sorry I don't recall anything about the move except doing what I was told to do. I don't remember our platoon getting into any type of fire at any time on that day. I do remember that we got word that the third platoon ran into a large force of either VC or N. V. A. I also remember picking up the pace of travel in order to get there to help out our brothers. Being a PFC I don't understand the war tactics at all, but I knew we had to get there as quickly as possible. I remember stopping a few times and wondering why we would do that when we had a whole platoon in trouble, but again I was just a PFC. I remember when we finally did get there we secured a perimeter around them and I can tell you that I didn't fire one single round that day and neither did anyone in my squad.

To this day I do feel bad for not getting to them any quicker than we did. I did not see any enemy at all that day, but that day will always be burned into my mind. The smell of death and the only thing left standing was the larger trees as far as I could see. I got behind a tree for cover and remember looking around the tree trunk and there were holes all around the tree. I remember thinking these poor men had no chance at all. I can only say that I was so sorry that we couldn't get there sooner. To this day I still apologize to them every time I say my prayers for not being able to do more.

I am a volunteer driver for the Disabled American Veterans. I take our brothers and sisters to their doctor appointments at VA hospitals and clinics. Our Altoona, PA Veterans Hospital has a wall just like the one in DC. Every time I go up there I go down to the wall and spend some time with the boys and again apologize for not being able to do more. I tell them that someday when the Lord calls me home I will spend some time with them and let them know that we did the best we could at the time.

This is what I remember of that awful day. I lost a lot of brothers and one special friend. Robert Michael Bowman and I went through basic training, AIT, and Jump School together. We hung out together every single minute we could after we got out of basic training. Got our first tats out in Salinas, CA. When we got to Vietnam we were split up. I went to first platoon and Bob went to third platoon. That was the last time I ever saw him alive. Still miss him a lot. Sorry I got off on another subject. That happens sometimes these days. But this is all I remember, Sir. I apologize for not doing better. I will see all of you at the reunion in June. Airborne!

PFC Bubber Fishbourne
Rifleman
1st Platoon
Manchester, GA

The following is from a letter that I wrote my Mom on July 2, 1966:

"Our company is in bad shape right now personnel wise. Choppers brought us to this area on the 29th of June. Soon after we landed, our 3rd Platoon was surrounded by a company of VC. My platoon was alerted soon after the 3rd Platoon encountered machine gun fire. The 3rd Platoon was calling over my radio that they needed help disparately.

We moved toward the 3rd Platoon immediately. My squad, the third squad, was fastest to begin the speedy movement.

Sgt Pomeroy was back in the states on emergency leave so we were under Sgt Showalter. There were 3 men ahead of me as we approached the firefight. A soldier named John, the second man in our squad, was killed instantly as a 30 cal round hit him in the cheek and went down into his chest. Sgt Showalter also caught a round, which ruined his shoulder. Sgt Jones was the medic tending to Sgt Showalter as I left him and advanced toward the position occupied by Morris and his Platoon Sgt. In our squad one of our boys has malaria, one has a broken foot and two have less than 30 days left. So they didn't come to the field with us.

As soon as we overcame the opposing force, we moved again. This time we had one more of our squad wounded. His wound was not serious, as he caught a bullet on his forehead that barely broke the skin.

The jungle in this area is so thick that we didn't bother to search for the enemy dead. The devils should have been buried I suppose but the crabs will eat them before they have a chance to run.

Soon we reached the 3rd Platoon and the sight was indescribable. I won't even try. If I could describe it like I saw it, you'd be as sick as I was.

It took all afternoon, and the next morning to load all the dead and wounded on helicopters.

When we began our march we were 90 men strong compared to what was reported to have been 200 VC. After we broke their camp and scattered them around the area we had 38 men left who were able to fight. Thank God we got the best of them.

My squad now has a total of four men left out of 12 starters. Already we received the word that 24 new men are back at base camp for replacements for our dead and wounded.

Tomorrow will be Independence Day at home, and tomorrow will be the same day here. I pray I won't hear one shot on July 4th. This will probably be a big story on the newscast. Listen for the 173rd's Operation Yorktown. Thanks for the Kool-Aid."

Sgt Jim Healy
Machine Gunner
3rd Platoon
Augusta, Maine

I know that this story does not fit in with what you are doing. But I'm on a roll and this is my favorite war story. Also, Sgt. Morris is my favorite combat NCO. His leadership style was quirky, unique, and invariably, right on target.

Charlie Morris joined the third Platoon of A 2/503 in early February 1966 as the squad leader of the weapons squad. He was a Korean War veteran, a no-nonsense "old school" NCO. He knew when not to get in your face and tell you were stupid, when you already knew you were stupid. And, he knew when to kick you in the ass, when you needed an ass kicking. He was a good NCO.

The third Platoon was the maneuver platoon on the 27th of February at Phu Loi. When the shit hit the fan, our platoon was to move around on the right flank and role up the left flank of the bad guys like an old newspaper. The gunfire was intense.

There was a lot of noise and a lot of confusion. As we moved around to the right, there was a lot of gunfire, and many explosions. By the time the third platoon got on the right and on line, there were only ten or fifteen of us. We did not surprise the bad guys. They knew we were there and they greeted us with the heaviest gunfire of my Vietnam experience. Twigs and branches were flying everywhere; small trees were being cut down by their "50's". It was intense.

I was a machine gunner. As my assistant gunner, Mac Holmes, and I got on line the gunfire from the bad guys intensified. I was surprised that any of us were still alive. We couldn't see the bad guys but we could sure feel the effects of their gunfire. Holmes and I began to return the fire. We fired low. Left to right and then back left again. If we couldn't roll up their flank, I was going to make damn sure that they didn't roll up ours.

The firing was continuous. I was sure no one could move without getting hit. Holmes and I just kept firing that M-60. Left to right, right to left. A couple of the guys around us got hit. We just kept working that M-60. Then, I caught a movement out of the corner of my eye. It was that new Sergeant—Sgt. Morris—and he was moving toward me. *What's that dumb shit doing?* I thought.

As I kept firing the machine gun I watched Sgt. Morris move closer and closer to me. He wasn't slithering under the leaves and brush, burrowing half under the ground, which was the only way I thought anyone could move without getting hit in the face of the incoming fire. He was moving in a formal, if there is such a thing, Army low crawl. His M-16 was cradled in his arms, his head was up, he was looking where he was going, straight toward me, and elbow, knee, elbow knee, he just kept moving toward me. *That dumb son-of-a-bitch is going to get shot!*, I thought. Elbow, knee, elbow, knee, he kept coming toward me. *If he's heading this way, risking his life, it must be to tell me something,* I thought. *Why the hell doesn't he just yell it out?* God knows there was plenty of yelling going on. Elbow, knee, elbow, knee, he just kept coming. *I must be missing something,* I thought. He must see something, I don't see. There is some target, some target of opportunity that I'm missing. I looked harder into the underbrush as I kept firing left to right, right to left. I couldn't see anything new. I kept firing and Sgt. Morris kept coming. Elbow, knee, elbow knee. Finally, he got up next to me. He was smiling. He was chewing on a cigar stub. He shoved his face up close to mine and said "Makes ya feel like you're in a real war don't it, Healy?" Then he turned and elbow, knee, elbow, knee headed back to his position. I can't remember Charlie Morris without thinking of this story. It still makes me smile today. What a magnificent NCO—what a magnificent man!

Sp4 Bob Lucas
Radio Telephone Operator (RTO)
2d Platoon
East Weymouth, Mass

I remember just as we landed at the designated LZ for the operation we ran into a LRRP unit. They ran to our chopper for their extraction. I talked to one of them and asked if they had seen anything. His reply was no contact but there were some footprints leading down

104

an old road. He also said that they found commo wire in the same area but never found the end of it.

After the choppers left the LZ we started to move through the area. I seem to remember that the platoons were to conduct what was called cloverleaf patrols. Not sure if anyone remembers that term being used. Not sure how far we moved or how long we were operating before we heard gunfire. It was a quick burst of shooting and then quiet. Within a minute or two it started again and this time it was relentless. You could hear machine guns, grenades, and everything between. The radio was going crazy. My call sign was 2 Alpha, 2nd Platoon, 1st Squad.

Third platoon had walked into a large element of gooks and was being chewed up pretty bad. The next thing I knew Capt. Kelley was calling everyone to move to the sound of the gunfire. Platoon Sergeant Nathaniel Brown led us to help save the 3rd Platoon and we were coming in from the left side of the battle. When we got within a 100-200 meters of the battle we were ambushed by an element of VC and hit the ground. I remember the battle was still raging and I could hear Capt. Kelley call for "2" (Sergeant Brown). I could see him from my position but figured his RTO was having trouble with his radio and couldn't hear anything. I called "6" and told him I could see "2" from my position. He quickly responded to get my ass over to "2" now. I did and landed to the left of Sgt. Brown. He looked at me and asked what in the hell was I doing? I told him "6" was on the radio and handed him my headset. He talked to "6" and told me to get back to my squad.

Sgt. Brown put the word out that we going to assault the enemy position that was firing at us. He wanted everyone online and when ready we stood up started shooting and walking to the enemy position. We drove them off and took their position. Sgt. Brown left a squad in their position and the rest of the Platoon ran to help 3rd Platoon. I remember the position must have been occupied by an enemy squad as they left all the gear in place and just ran away.

When we got to the 3rd platoon the 1st platoon was here and securing the area and giving first aid. We did the same, but the situation was not good. There were many bodies laid out in tight groups of four or five guys.

Pfc James Miskel
Rifleman
3rd Platoon
Boston, MA

Once we landed on the LZ and left the company assembly area the 3rd platoon moved out to the West. It was the normal jungle terrain and all was well to start with, but later we discovered a creek in the area that had enemy positions, and they opened fire. We were hit with AK 47 fire, machine gun fire, and what I thought was a 57mm recoilless rifle that hit one of our guys, Doc Berry, and knocked his shoulder off. Our machinegun team was one of the two in our platoon, and our gun was rendered inoperable when an enemy round hit it and knocked it out of action. We picked up M-16s from the casualties near us and returned fire, and I saw the platoon RTO get hit. He survived as well as Plt Sgt Cooney who was also WIA. We were surrounded.

I heard cries from one of our wounded and crawled to help him. He was dead and I told one of the guys not to talk because the enemy was directing their fire whenever they heard voices. Another one of our team was hit and we got some plastic to cover the wound and help stop the bleeding; it was Palmer I believe. I crawled back to my position. My team, which included the gunner, myself (I was the assistant gunner), and two other guys, did survive the battle.

When the rest of the company got there the first friendly face I saw was one of our guys from the Weapons Platoon. Glad to see him!

PFC Bill Palmer
Rifleman/Ammo Bearer
3rd Platoon
Dayton, Ohio

I remember the barrel of the 60 glowing red, and the difficult time we had changing it. It was also about this time that a burst of gunfire hit between me and, I believe, Simmons on my right. From the angle the tracer rounds came in, it was obviously to our rear and high; like it came from in the trees. As I turned and probably came up to more of a sitting position to look up, I was immediately hit in the back, probably from a position directly in front of us.

While I remained in control, I was stunned by the impact and knew I was in trouble. Every time I took a breath the air was escaping through the opening in my back and making a gurgling sound. My life was probably saved by Pfc James Miskell who managed to find a large piece of plastic wrapping and tightly secured that over the opening in my back making it easier to breath. While weak and bleeding a lot, I was able to continue firing my weapon at muzzle flashes or

107

movement. I never did clearly see the enemy, although they were close. I later learned that I was hit twice by (probably) a 30-caliber machine gun. Both bullets had punctured my right lung and both hit ribs, fracturing them but keeping the bullets from exiting which the doctors felt contributed to my survival. I remember at some point being very low on ammunition and believe we marked our position with smoke and additional ammo was dropped by helicopter. (I might have been a little out of it by this point and dreamed this, but it remains a memory). I do clearly remember the Viet Cong yelling "die Americans, die" as they probed *and* attacked our positions. I remember Sgt. Morris yelling back at them. One thing I have always been amazed at was the discipline of the platoon in maintaining composure and continuing the fight despite knowing we would probably be overrun; thankfully they were never able to break through.

Once help arrived I was moved to an area that was somewhat clear, and then lifted out in a wire basket by an Air Force rescue helicopter. Due to the amount of blood loss I was first transported to a field hospital and stabilized. From there I was moved to a hospital in Saigon for a couple of days, then on to Japan where I remained in the hospital until Sep. 16th. I returned to the 173rd on the 17th, but was assigned to HHC. I returned to the states in mid-April of '67. I was assigned to the 82nd where I completed my tour. I still remember fairly clearly the firefight on the 29th and some of the nighttime ambush patrols I was involved in, but do not remember a lot of detail from other less intense engagements. I have always been extremely proud to have served with the 173rd.

Ron Sedlack
Rifleman, 3rd Platoon
Corunna, MI

At the time of this story I was 20-years old. I received my draft papers and went to serve my country as my grandfather had in World War I and my father in World War II. My father was a tail gunner on a B17. He was a decorated war hero. This is the story of a teenage boy who left the states and returned a man.

At the time of this story I was a PFC, and later promoted to Sgt. I chose to go airborne and was assigned to the 173rd Airborne Brigade in Viet Nam—a special brigade of paratroopers. I was assigned to the 2nd battalion, 503rd infantry, A company, 3rd platoon, 3rd squad with, Sergeant Morris as my squad leader.

I arrived in Viet Nam in March of 1966. Initially I was in a holding camp near Saigon, and the first night the camp was mortared, and the reality of war set in. This was real. There were numerous casualties. The horror is etched in my mind as I heard men crying for help and dying. I closed my eyes and thought of the dozens of coffins at the airfield waiting to go home. I was so scared. I wondered if I would ever see the United States again.

We trucked out to Bien Hoa the next day, which was near the airbase. This was to be my new home in this country. This was the home of the *Third Herd* (so called because the commanding general played Rawhide as reveille in the morning). It was a big tent city. There were approximately twenty men, or two squads, in a tent. We slept on cots covered with mosquito nets because of all the insects at the edge of the jungle where the camp was situated.

Upon arrival at the camp, I met Sgt. Morris, my squad leader. He informed me that I had midnight guard duty that night. The following story is dedicated to those GIs who made the supreme sacrifice with their young lives on June 29, 1966, and to those of us who were lucky enough to survive. It is about men who were not afraid to serve their country. They reflect the patriotism and pride that lives in our country today, with the freedom to make choices, and speak freely as is also reflected in our constitution.

I was awakened about 1:00 am on that morning to the sound of Sgt. Morris screaming at me, "Why the hell aren't you on guard duty?" He jerked me out of my cot and slammed a rifle in my hands. I thought, *My God, what have I done?* Sgt. Morris marched me out to the perimeter to the guard post where I was introduced to a black trooper who had less than 30 days left to go in The Nam. I am sorry to say that I don't recall his name, but I do remember how weary and tired he looked. I wondered how 1 would look if I survived that long—a tour of duty 12 months long.

Sgt. Morris quizzed him as to why I was not awakened for guard duty. The trooper informed him that he did not want a nervous cherry newbie (a common nickname for new men in the country) getting him killed with less than 30 days left in The Nam. His comment made me more frightened, especially of not being able to do what I had been trained to do.

Infantry troopers in Viet Nam were referred to as "grunts," and for a very good reason. We carried a lot of gear and humped the jungles like pack animals. We carried a rucksack with personal belongings, extra socks, smokes, and C-rats. We carried approximately 20 magazines of ammo for our

M-16's, extra belts of ammo, a bayonet, 2 smoke grenades, and at least 4 or more frags (high output fragmentation grenades). In addition to this, some troopers carried a blooper, which was an M-79 grenade launcher, along with the ammo. Some troopers carried pistols and ammo. Most troopers carried an M-16 as their major weapon. The M-60 was assigned to two men, a gunner and an assistant. There were two of these per platoon. A platoon was four squads of about 40 men. Some troopers chose to carry additional weapons of their choice. Frequently they carried shotguns and ammo for close fighting, pistols, and extra ammo belts for the machine guns. Numerous men carried LAW (light anti tank weapon). A LAW was a tube with a small rocket in it, and was electronically ignited when fired. This weapon was very effective for knocking out bunkers in the jungle. Most troopers carried a pack of C-4, a plastic explosive, which when used with a detonator is a powerful explosive. Each squad had a sergeant squad leader and a fire team leader who led half the squad. A squad was about 10 men. Each platoon had a platoon sergeant and a platoon leader who was a second lieutenant.

We had received word of a Viet Cong regiment thought to be operating in the Xaun Loc area according to LRP (long range patrol) reports. The second battalion was going to look for them. We were sent out in company size units, and A Company was chosen to break up into platoon-sized units to search the area. The rationale for this decision was that we could better cover more area than an entire company, which is usually assigned to such a task.

When we found out that we were being split into platoons, and choppered out to our AO (area of operation). I became very nervous, my guts were in knots and I was smoking nonstop. We were about a thousand meters from each of the other platoons (a total of four platoons was in this operation).

This meant that if we were to stumble onto Charlie in the dense jungle it would be a long time before backup help would be able to reach us.

June 27 choppers put down in the LZ (landing zone), which were to be our search areas. We exited the choppers and headed into the dense jungles. By mid afternoon the heat of the jungle was sweltering and oppressive. We were ringing wet, as usual, beneath our gear as we humped the jungle looking for Charlie. We stopped for our night lager (bivouac) area at the edge of the jungle near a rubber plantation. A rubber plantation is rows of rubber trees, similar to a fruit orchard in the states; the difference is that rubber trees are a lot taller. There are hundreds of these plantations dotting the Viet Nam landscape. I was thinking how hard it was to believe that my country relied on this country for rubber until nylon tires came out the 50s.

We set up our perimeter and settled in for the night. Part of preparing for the night included digging a foxhole to sleep in for the night. The size of a foxhole depended on whether one or two men were sharing it. At night you wrapped yourself in your poncho. It's hard to imagine that after the sweltering heat of the day that 70-80 degrees felt chilly. We took turns on guard duty at night even though the night enveloped us in an inky black darkness. Most of the nights you couldn't see anything in the dark

I was located in a foxhole near the edge of the jungle by myself, because my partner had contracted malaria. It was not uncommon to contract this disease in the jungle. Many of the troopers carried hammocks with them, which they would string between trees at night because of all the wonderful creepy crawly things indigenous to the jungle night. It's difficult to sleep under these conditions, especially when you are frightened. One finds himself not really sleeping, but

112

catnapping. You try not to stir or make any unnecessary noise. In the middle of the night I was startled awake with a thought of hearing something. It was nothing at all except the dense blackness of the jungle night. After a few minutes I pulled my poncho over my head and had a smoke, and then drifted back off to sleep.

I was awakened at daybreak by numerous explosions and the screaming of wounded men. I could hear cries for the medic. I saw our medic, Malcolm Berry, who was a tall black young man heading for the wounded. He was from New Jersey, full of life and fun to be around—a good friend. *My God we're being mortared!* As I observed the scene from my foxhole, the explosions were around the area of the rubber trees. Two troopers died in their hammocks, three others were wounded. Suddenly everything became quiet. We ventured slowly out of our foxholes. They called in dust offs (medevac choppers) to carry out the wounded, and we were left with 36 men in our platoon. What a helluva way to start the day! I was soon to learn that this was Charlie's way of waking us up.

It's June 28th, and the rest of the day proves to be uneventful. We stopped for our night lager area. We were a weary, tired group of GIs this night. We were awakened the morning of June 29th with the sun filtering through the jungle, and as we broke up our morning bivouac and headed for the jungles, we had no clue as to the danger lurking ahead.

After approximately 20 minutes, to an hour, we were approaching a swampy area. I noticed how deathly quiet the jungle seemed this morning. It didn't register with me at the time that this was unusual. As we marched forward in single file, I was about three quarters back in the platoon. Suddenly we came to a stop and dropped to a kneeling position, with every other man facing the outside (every other man facing the opposite direction). Sgt. Morris went ahead to the point people who had stumbled onto some blue commo wire, as well as other discard from the enemy, including a slit trench (latrine).

Sgt. Morris and Leslie Smith advanced forward cautiously following the commo wire. An enemy 30-caliber machine gun opened fire on them at point blank range. Both men were hit and went down. Sgt. Morris was hit in the chest. He rolled over and raised up spotting a Chinese advisor, in his own words he, "shot the slope bastard in the head"

The machine gum continued firing. Sgt. Morris threw in a grenade and blew up the rest of the gun crew. Barry, our medic, moved forward to bring Sgt. Morris and Smith back. By now heavy arms fire was all along our front. Under a hail of gunfire, Barry, Smith and Sgt. Morris made it back to our line. Barry started to administer first aid to Smith and Morris. Smith would later die. Sgt. Morris had a serious chest wound, but refused to stop fighting.

The rest of the platoon formed an immediate perimeter. We were now under very, very heavy gunfire. As I moved forward to my position, I felt a searing pain in my right hip. I was later to learn that I had a flesh wound. At that point my only thought was to get into position and start firing. As I settled into a position in a swampy area, I heard a 50-caliber machine gun open fire, and I thought, *My God they must be really dug in to have a 50 caliber machine gun.*

We were on the right flank of the front of the perimeter. Sgt. Richard Hido was on my left and Ed Ball was on the Sgt's left. On my right was Ferguson and Shasteen with an M60 machine gun. Sgt. Fritz was down from them on their right. We could now hear several machine guns firing and a helluva lot of AK47s (a Russian rifle the Viet Cong used, which was very effective). Grenades were dropping all around us. All you could hear over the sounds of the explosives were the screams of the wounded calling for the medic.

We were later to learn that we had stumbled onto the Viet Cong base camp with an estimated strength of over 500 men. Our platoon sergeant, Sgt. Cooney, was in the middle of the platoon by a tree. He had been wounded and was hysterical. The RTO (radio operator) lay dead beside him. They had made contact with the other platoons, who were starting a forward march to our position. Sgt. Cooney was screaming for a radio. Mike Thibault, our FO (forward observer for artillery), was on the lead flank towards the front. He was calling for air support, which was unavailable, and artillery, which for some unknown reason we never received. He called for gunships (specially armed helicopters), which also never arrived. He later took his radio back to Sgt. Cooney who was still hysterically hollering. Thibault had been shot in the shoulder and he dropped his radio off to Sgt. Cooney. As Mike got up to move to a better position, he was gut shot.

Paul Surette, who was a close friend of mine from Boston, and Francis Stevens, another close friend, being close to the front, were both killed in a deadly crossfire. We were now completely surrounded, with gunfire pouring in from all sides. With machine guns sweeping the area everything was destroyed. They leveled every bit of underbrush in their path. I, like everyone else, was concentrating on keeping up our firepower, shooting at movement and muzzle flashes. The enemy mounted an assault on our position, which we drove off. By now our medic, Malcolm Barry, had been shot in the leg, as he tended to the wounded. Sgt. Morris, despite his own serious wounds, was trying to care for the wounded and keep up the battle.

The gunfire was so heavy that I swear you could have walked on the lead between the two lines. By now our only thoughts were concentrating on getting out of there alive. The urge to survive took away the fear. I thought to myself; *My God, how many of them are out there?* A grenade had knocked out our M60 machine gun on the left flank. Billy Taylor was badly wounded; Sgt. Morris saved his life by tending his wounds and calming him down. Marshall sustained serious wounds to his arm and his leg. He would later lose part of each of his injured extremities. He survived due to Sgt. Morris applying tourniquets to his injured limbs. Sgt. Morris moved among the alive and wounded calming them down and encouraging them to keep fighting. Malcolm Barry was giving him advice on how to handle the wounded when someone else screamed for a medic. As Malcolm moved to his position, he was fatally wounded. He would receive a Silver Star medal posthumously.

I heard cursing and swearing on my right flank. As I crawled over to see what was wrong, I realized that I did not hear the 60 firing. As I reached their position, Fergie cried out, "The machine gun is jammed up!" Shasteen was on his hands and knees with a cigarette hanging out of his mouth, field stripping the gun to fix it. Fergie was lying on his back with a pistol across his chest hollering for him to hurry up. Shasteen reassembled the 60, put a belt in it and started firing,

The Viet Cong came at our position again, and once more we were able to drive them back. Shasteen was shot through the leg, and Sgt. Fritz was hit in the chest. He was in serious condition. (Sgt. Fritz did not even have to be there, having a father who was a Colonel serving in Viet Nam). We realized that he was mortally wounded and watched helplessly as he lay dying. He began screaming out loud asking God to spare his life. It was very unnerving and painful listening to him beg God not to let him die, and knowing that there was nothing you could do to help him. Little did I know that I would carry

116

the memory of Sgt. Fritz's death with me for the rest of my life. Each time he cried out, the Viet Cong would concentrate heavy fire in his area. We tried to keep him calm and quiet until he died in anguish. Sgt. Morris continued to move about the perimeter, checking positions and gathering ammo from the dead to give to the living.

He now realized that they had set up a machine gun behind us. Sgt. Morris went back by Jones' position. Jones was shot up on the left side, and as Sgt Morris assisted him, Jones told him he could still fire with his one hand. Sgt. Morris went out of the perimeter to knock out the machine gun, and in doing so received yet another wound. When Morris crawled back to Jones' position, Jones lay dead.

Numerous times Sgt. Morris would yell, "Die, you commie bastards!" In response, the Viet Cong would holler insults back to us. There were still a lot of grenades going off inside our perimeter thrown by the Viet Cong. We could also hear them popping tubes and dropping mortars on us. Sgt. Morris even said he saw them firing RPG (rocket power grenades) at us. An explosion went off close to my left and I heard Sgt. Hido screaming, "My God I'm hit! My arm! My arm!" I crawled over to his position thinking he might need a tourniquet, and as I reached him, I thought, *oh my God!* Because his arm was blown completely off and lying about 10 feet away. All I could see was a hole with ribs sticking out, as he looked up at me and said, "Please help me find my arm." He then died.

As I crawled back to my position, I heard a machine gun open fire and I felt the bullets tear through my left shoulder and across my back as I had partially exposed myself. As I reached up at the hole in my back I began to think that none of us would get out of there alive. I must have screamed out when I was hit, because Ed Ball came over to assess my injuries. As Ed put a field dressing on my wound I could see by the look in his eyes that he figured I was done for. As he crawled away, Ed was shot through the buttocks.

On the left another explosion occurred. Sgt. Potter was hit. Both arms were blown off and he died. The unrelenting Viet Cong tried another assault, which we drove off. Sgt. Morris, among his wounds, had a badly wounded hand and could not pull the pin on the grenade. His thumb was good, so he pulled the grenade pins with his thumb. He had such a big thumb that by the end of the firefight he had seven pins hanging on his thumb.

I felt pain in my right chest and realized that I had been hit again. Ed Ball, lying on my left flank firing his M16, a bullet tore through the casing on the rifle, peppering my face with shrapnel. Ed, cursing, threw the rifle down and crawled over to get Sgt. Hido's rifle. I was getting weaker, barely able to squeeze the trigger, let alone reload my rifle.

We could hear the enemy talking and yelling, and figured they were getting ready for another attack. We began to realize that with our casualties we could no longer hold them back. We had been in continuous combat for almost ten hours. *When was this going to end?* Then the gunfire started to let up some. So many grenades had gone off in the perimeter that everyone sustained shrapnel wounds. Sgt. Morris had been wounded five times.

First and Second platoons were getting closer and moving in behind the Viet Cong. As Second Platoon reached the Viet Cong perimeter, the platoon leader lined them up and they charged the hill, firing their weapons as they came, driving away the remaining Viet Cong.

As I lay face down in the swamp, weak from the loss of blood, and listening to the assault, I thought, *The bastards are coming again.* I didn't realize that the gunfire was coming away from our position. Weakened from blood loss, I pulled the pin on my last grenade with it underneath me and passed out. My rationale was that if they roll my body over the grenade would go off killing several more.

The second platoon made it into our perimeter. They witnessed the ghastly horror of dead and wounded everywhere. Thirteen troopers gave their all that day. Thirteen heroes! Most of the survivors had been wounded two or three times. Lt. Voss was checking to see who was dead and who was alive. He observed Sgt. Morris lying among the dead, not moving. He kicked Sgt. Morris in the foot and was shocked when he opened his eyes. As he leaned over Sgt. Morris, the Sgt. reached up and grabbed his fatigue jacket and told him to be sure to get the more seriously wounded evacuated out first. Sgt. Morris was awarded the Congressional Medal of Honor for his valor on this day.

Ed Ball was being taken out with the wounded, and he glanced over and saw me lying with blood on my face and thought I was dead. I vaguely remember a medic saying, "My God this one is still alive with a grenade in his hand."

Because of the swamps they could not make an LZ for the dust offs. The air force sent in a different kind of chopper with baskets to remove the rest of the wounded to MASH units where we were patched up so we could be transferred to larger field hospitals.

As I waited for evacuation via basket I looked around and saw Surrett and Stevens, my buddies, as they lay lifeless. It was the end of dear friendships. Both soldiers lay with their rifle in their arms, the upper hand now supporting their heads. They looked like they had just lain down and were taking a nap with their rifles. As I surveyed the area around me, my gaze rested on

119

the sight of Sgt. Hido's body and Sgt. Fritz's body on the other side. Everyone was covered with blood. Reality was taking over. *Why did God let me live?* I felt guilty as I fought to remain conscious. I was so scared, and vaguely remember being put in the basket for evacuation. I then lost consciousness.

My next memory was awakening in the field hospital, bandaged and taped up with IVs running in my arms. I first thought was, *My God, I am alive! I made i*t! My moment of elation ended as the horror and deadly reality of what happened set in. How many times would I relive this memory? I still remember the MASH unit, exactly like the weekly MASH TV series. I couldn't believe it when I saw Sgt. Morris, despite his own injuries, dressed in clean fatigues and walking tall. If you didn't know, you would never guess that he was wounded too. He checked on each of us to see how we were doing, and if we needed anything. He did have his hand all bandaged up.

When I reflect on that day, I always think of Sgt Morris. Sgt. Morris was a true hero in the tradition of Sgt. York and Audie Murphy. He didn't think he had done anything special; let alone extraordinary. He would say, "I was just helping you guys out. Your combined efforts are what kept us going." When President Johnson awarded him the Medal of Honor, he said, "This belongs to the guys who were with me. They are the ones who really deserve this, not me; they supported me. I just helped them out." His words just reinforce what a true hero he really was.

Men in a different position may have witnessed additional or different experiences on the day, June 29, 1966. The day, and the events, is permanently etched in my mind. It would be thirty years before any of the survivors were to see each other again, and share the events of the day when thirteen heroes gave their young lives for their country.

PFC Mike Sturges
Rifleman
3rd Platoon

Our Squad Leader was either Sgt Fritts or Sgt Hido. Don't recall anything significant about the move from the base camp to the PZ- did hear the mortars- and thought, *That's a hell of a way to start the day.* No thoughts of the airlift or the move to the LZ and to Co A's position. Once we moved forward out of the Co A's area to the West we were the last squad in the Platoon. Later we encountered a few shots at first, then silence, and then a few more, and then all hell broke loose. We were taking fire from all directions there was a 50 cal MG off to the right raking us. I had the M-79 guy put rounds on it and it seemed to stop. Where we were there was no real cover.

Shasteen and I noticed some trees forward and crawled towards them and encountered trenches and a bunker. We then came under heavy fire and had to pull back. There were lots of wounded including Fritts and Hido. I worked on them both as I recall. I remember someone else saying "it's getting darker", and then he died.

The fire picked up and we had MG, RPG, mortars and grenades coming at us and what seemed like a big orange football; not sure what that was. I was spending time pulling bodies back to a mound where there were already a lot of bodies. We were just about out of ammo, I recall redistributing ammo and taking dressings off the dead to use on the live wounded and I recall patching up Sgt Morris .The RTO was killed, and I had heard someone around the radio saying, "if they hit us once more we're all dead". We then formed a small perimeter, and discussed what we'd do if we were about to be captured. Then I saw a GI helmet coming towards us and…it was Woody Davis of the 1st Platoon!

I had been hit in the foot, but it was not bad enough to be lifted out that evening. The next day the Bn Cdr helo dropped a rope and they placed me in a body bag and lifted me up and out to a cleared area some distance away. They let me down there and moved me to a Dust Off then flew me to an Evac Hospital in Saigon.

Lt Vendetti with MSG Pigeon, PLT SGT

1st Lt Gus Vendetti
Weapons Platoon Leader
3rd Platoon
Townline, NY

The Battle of June 29, 1966 for me started June 28th at 1200 Hours. Our unit went in on the 28th and started securing the area for the 2d Bn perimeter. We set up and monitored roadblocks, letting the local Vietnamese through the checkpoints. In hindsight, we didn't know who they were. In retrospect some VC knew our position and successfully fired a mortar (others said used grenades) into our area, killing Felder and Graves. They also wounded two others, one of whom was Clover.

Once we made the airmobile assault onto LZ Brazil the three rifle platoons were ordered to recon to the west. We were told to be 1000 meters apart. The Weapons Platoon and

122

Headquarters were to remain near the LZ and be prepared to act as the reserve. When the battle started the 1,000 meters apart proved to be a mistake because the dense jungle and the hilly terrain made it hard to help the 3rd Platoon, which took the worst of the battle.

I was the 1st Lt of 3rd Platoon, but was switched to the Weapons Platoon because they needed an Officer. Lt. Algood, who was in charge, was wounded on June 26th and evacuated. SSgt Cooney took charge of 3rd Platoon in my absence. Weapons Plt was with HQ when we moved west to help the 3rd Plt. While in the process of doing this we received a call from Capt. Kelley that all units were to help 3rd Platoon because it was taking heavy fire. Weapons, which was with the 2nd Platoon, had just come upon a VC position which was about 8 foot higher than the surrounding area, and where there was a 50 Cal and two 30 Cal machine guns set up. The 50 and one 30cal were abandoned but the other 30 cal was firing at 3rd Platoon's position. We started taking on fire ourselves and moved off the hill where guns were set up to obtain some cover. I then radioed 1st Platoon leader, Bill Vose, and told him where the firing was coming from. First Platoon took the 30 cal out and his platoon ended the heavy fire.

The VC were bugging out. Weapons Plt continued toward 3rd Platoon's position. The jungle was thick and I noticed that the VC had cut channels in the foliage to obtain a better advantage of getting eyes on us. The area smelled of urine, gunpowder and smoke. As we approached 3rd Platoon, we came upon many wounded and dead. It was a horrible scene. The area smelled again of urine, gunpowder, smoke and now blood. Body parts were all over. Very few of the dead were VC. I believe I only saw two dead VC. These were sights and sounds I would never forget. We came upon Charlie Morris and he was shot five times and still had all the grenade rings on his finger. I stayed with the dead and remember laying our deceased comrades in a more dignified manner because it really bothered me to see them in the awkward positions. Recall, just days before this had been my platoon. These were men I had just been talking to and it really hurt and does to this day. That evening and the next morning all KIA and WIA were lifted out of the thick jungle by Dust Off helicopters, regular helicopters with ropes or cargo nets, Air Force helicopters and CH47's. I have always felt like the Intel should have been better so as to know what we were marching into. But hindsight is 20/20.

Lt. Bill Vose
Platoon Leader
1st Platoon
Miami, FL

Moving to the LZ we were mortared. The mortars landed just about on our heads, right on first platoon. We were guarding the hilltop (we were part of the Battalion security perimeter) that overlooked the path from the village that the mortars came from. One KIA. Felder never got up for stand-to and was still in a hammock sleeping and mortar round blew his foot off and he bled out.

Other WIAs we were patching them up and putting fire onto the village when the CO called up yelling at me to saddle up and get to the LZ and get on choppers, I told him I was in contact and had wounded. I was then ordered to leave those who couldn't move to be attended to and to didi mau to the LZ.

We had not broken down C's yet so I had NCOs gather up troops and left the severely wounded (1 or 2 don't remember) and ran to the choppers. I then called in 4.2 on the Ville which struck (WP) the village as we took off. It was my present for Felder!

Timing: 1st platoon, upon hearing fire from 3d Platoon's area, we were hunkered down breaking down C's and getting gear together. Upon hearing fire I saddled up the platoon and within 2-3 minutes we were fast walking directly to the sound of the guns. I only got on Radio once I can remember, wasn't monitoring too busy, but I heard you talking to SSgt Cooney, and I got him and said we were close and expect us soon...we then encountered 12.7. We dropped packs. I left one man to guard and put the platoon online with two m60s in center and we massed fire and it ended the enemy firing. We then proceeded a few more minutes and were sloshing through this grey mud/muck for a while. We then came to red streaks in the gray mud and it was the third platoon's...we found them all gray and covered in the mud, but really smiling when they saw us. We made a perimeter and starting rendering first aid. I went to Cooney who was shot in the ass.

I encountered Morris with the 2 sucking chest wounds and thumbs full of grenade pins. I don't remember when the other platoon got there. It seemed like hours, as we were all exhausted from the run, the adrenalin of battle and then the comedown after. We then requested chainsaws that were dropped and cut a hole in triple canopy to get out wounded.

As a note: When Thibault, Sturges, and I went back to this battle site in 1999 it had all been cleared and was a rice paddy now. The bunker was still there. You could see it but not get to it. We have a film of it! As for the enemy? We were able to talk to a local VC commander on our return trip.

PFC Warren Weissenbacher
Rifleman
3rd Platoon
Niles, CA

My name is Warren Weissenbacher (MOS-11B1P), and five of us new guys (Wright, Wheeler, myself, and two others) were replacements for 3rd platoon on June 30th. It was quite an introduction to A Co. Our first day joining A Co. at the base camp in Bien Hoa we were told to report to the 3rd Plt area. When we got there a Sgt took us to the 3rd platoon area which was an old large canvas tents, He told us to throw our duffel bags into one of the tents and a chopper would be by soon to take us out to where the 3rd Plt was. We were in our nice new jungle fatigues and had no other gear. The Sgt said don't worry about it, you'll get some. Less than an hour later the chopper arrived and flew us way out into some jungle area and dropped us off. A Sgt came out of the jungle and said to follow him. He took us to a large pile of rucksacks, pistol belts, M-16's, canteens, helmets and said to pick out the equipment we needed. Some of the stuff was messed up, damaged, we noticed bullet holes and some dried blood and we realized this gear was

126

from the 3rd Plt firefight the day before. No personal items were in this gear. So now our pucker factor was way up there!

After we suited up and went into the 3rd Plt area, some of the guys all pretty dirty and rough looking, looked at us new guys in our clean jungle fatigues and wearing their buddies gear. They just kind of rolled their eyes at us.

That night, our first night with 3rd Plt, we were in a Company perimeter and 3rd Plt had a fairly open area and sloping down from us had trip flares, claymores out, and our prone shelters dug. The powers-that-be must have been worried we would be hit that night. They choppered in supplies and a 50 cal machine gun that we set up on our perimeter.

Some people look at me strange when I say sometimes there can be humor in combat. In the middle of the night a single VC sneaking in tripped a trip flare, was standing about 50 meters out. We sat up, and he dove down and we all opened up. The 50 cal, two M-60's and all our M-16's. Must have sounded like World War II. John Wayne would have been proud. The rest of the company probably thought we were being overrun. One Sgt hollered to cease fire and he was busting out laughing. He told the mortar crews on the radio to try and hold out and they would lay down fire out front of us. So we all had a big laugh. Just one VC, and guess what? We found no body or blood trail the next day. He had dropped into a depression and is probably still running! I think that broke the ice with us and the old timers.

As a final note; I'm very proud of 98% of the guys I served with. They served with honor and courage. I also had the honor to meet and speak with Sgt Morris years later. What a humble and great man he was. Thomas Taylor, who survived the June 29th firefight, had his M-60 shot up but he wasn't hit, and after a time I went to his M-60 crew and when he was a short timer. I took over his M-60 and had the privilege of making the combat jump on Feb 22, 1967 with it— canvas bag strapped to my leg.

Part Five

Serving with Heroes–Marching with Giants

The American Military has dozens of medals that can be awarded for performance or participation in various endeavors, but only a small handful, known as "valor awards," are given for acts of courage. The highest and most revered of these is the Medal of Honor. According to military regulations, the Medal of Honor is awarded to a soldier who performed a deed of "personal bravery" that was "beyond the call of duty" and "involved risk of life."

Sgt Charles Morris has gone down in American history as one of those few–one in a million few–to be awarded the Medal of Honor. He was the point squad leader of the 3rd Platoon that hit the enemy battalion on June 29, 1966 was hit with enemy fire repeatedly. At the end of the fight he would be the Platoon Leader. Some reports had him with 33 wounds. The witness statements that day listed his valor in eliminating machine gun emplacements, becoming the medic when Doc Berry was killed, working with Mike Thibault on adjusting artillery fire, repeatedly moving out to assist wounded, and encouraging the men of his platoon while being seriously wounded himself. Words about his actions that day are many. Each member of that platoon who survived and remained (13 in all) had a different story; each telling of *heroism, concern, encouragement,* and *professionalism.* For one composite re-look of that day and what this soldier did, one needs only to read the citation for the decoration Charlie Morris received…for *"conspicuous gallantry and intrepidity at the risk of life, above and beyond the call of duty"* . . . the *Medal of Honor.*

Here is Sgt Morris' open letter about receiving the Medal of Honor. It is followed by his enclosure of the complete citation:

"To begin with I can tell you that we were in the vicinity of Xuan Loc (Swan Loc) searching for major VC-NVA units known to be in that area. The 11th Armored Cavalry Regiment was scheduled to come to that area in the summer. They were coming directly from the States. Our mission was to drive out the bad guys until the 11th ACR could move in and prepare to defend themselves. Why was a lonely platoon out there looking for hundreds of bad guys? I'm afraid that the answer is that the Army is always willing to sacrifice a few good men to gain information that might save the lives of hundreds. As I remember the operation, we operated at battalion strength then split up into companies going off in separate directions. When this failed in making contact we then were inserted by companies and split into separate platoons—each going in different directions.

The 3rd Platoon A Co 2-503 made the contact that everyone was looking for. I was later told that the unit we hit was a Main Force VC Battalion. (I no longer remember the number of the unit). From the uniforms and equipment they were carrying I can say they were a very well equipped, heavily armed unit. I am also sure that they had Chinese or Manchurian advisors since I shot a big ugly SOB in the face at less than 10 ft.

We were so shot up that we couldn't prevent them from carrying off all of their casualties and military junk. When we made contact, Smith and I were out on point and were the first people hit. The first burst of fire came from a machine gun not more than 50 ft. away. That gun was so well hidden that I could only find it by the muzzle flash when it fired. Smith and I rejoined the platoon and then the fight really started. When the VC opened up with everything they had we knew we were in over our heads, and in a world of shit. Doc Berry was hit early as were several others but those who could, kept firing until they were hit again and disabled or killed. (For my actions) I did receive the Medal of Honor but did nothing heroic that I remember. I was a rifleman, a medic (Doc Berry died), a grenadier, a leader and anything else that I was able to do. I did get hit by 5 bullets and at least a dozen grenade, mortar, or rocket fragments, but hell, anyone can do that…especially if he leaves his ass hanging out. At the end of the day A Company got to us but the fight was over. The VC had pulled out.

The remains of the Company searched for VC in the area for several days and could smell dead bodies but never found them. The 3d Platoon was hurt bad. We had 13 dead and 26 wounded. I anticipate your question of why we didn't haul ass instead of staying to fight. If we had run, we would have had to leave our dead and seriously wounded friends behind. We were paratroopers, and know that we stay together.

A little about myself: I stayed in the army for 15 more years finally retiring as a Sergeant Major. (I'm not sure if I'm a retarded Sergeant Major, or a retired Sergeant Major.) I never publicized my Medal of Honor. It is very personal to me since it represented the guys I was with. Some may even be more deserving, but I was chose for some reason. I will not write my story. I will not sell anything to the TV and movie vultures, even though I had a few minor offers. I have had contact with our former company commander, Jack Kelley, and a few others from the 173rd but I prefer to be left alone. I attended the 173rd convention in Sacramento in 1994 and I plan to go to the convention this year. For me that is a big change since I hadn't attended a convention in over 20 years.

Since my retirement in 81' I haven't done anything important. I spent some time in school. I spent many thousands of miles on a motorcycle and could be found around the racetracks all over the east coast. I did work with a very high tech security outfit at Delta Force and Joint Special Operations Command for several years and that was really interesting. Now I'm retired for the second time and slowly getting old, fat, and grandfatherly. You might remember that I was 34 years old in 1966 so I guess it is time I start to act my age. I do shoot a lot now (pistols) but do not hunt. I also take time to remember good men from the past. I have not attempted to correct my spelling, paragraphing or punctuation but I make no apology, and hope you can recognize my sincerity.

For your information I have enclosed a copy for the citation for the Medal of Honor. I never add to or deny the official version of our actions. Each of us saw different things that day. The only brag that I ever make is that I was a soldier. I hope that you too look back with pride to your days in uniform. I hope I have answered a few questions from a day in your past. For the future I wish you good health and may you spend your life in peace.

SSGT Charles Morris
Squad Leader / Rifleman / Platoon Leader
3rd Platoon, 2/503rd Airborne Infantry, 173rd Airborne Brigade
Carrol County, VA

The President of the United States of America, authorized by Act of Congress, March 3, 1863, has awarded in the name of The Congress the Medal of Honor to

Staff Sergeant (then Sergeant) Charles B. Morris,
United States Army

for conspicuous gallantry and intrepidity in action at the risk of his life above and beyond the call of duty:

While on a search and destroy mission in the Republic of Vietnam on 29 June 1966, Sergeant Morris was a leader of the point squad of a platoon of Company A, 2nd Battalion, 503rd Infantry. Seeing indications of the enemy's presence in the area, Sergeant Morris deployed his squad and continued forward alone to make a reconnaissance. He unknowingly crawled within 20 meters of an enemy machine gun, whereupon the gunner fired, wounding him in the chest. Sergeant Morris instantly returned the fire and killed the gunner. Continuing to crawl within a few feet of the gun, he hurled a grenade and killed the remainder of the enemy crew. Although in pain and bleeding profusely, Sergeant Morris continued his reconnaissance. Returning to the platoon area, he reported the results of his reconnaissance to the platoon leader. As he spoke the platoon came under heavy fire. Refusing medical attention for himself, he deployed his men in better firing positions confronting the entrenched enemy to his front. Then for eight hours the platoon engaged the numerically superior enemy force. Withdrawal was impossible without abandoning many wounded and dead. Finding the platoon "medic" dead, Sergeant Morris administered first aid to himself, and was returning to treat the wounded members of his squad with the "medic's" first aid kit when he was again wounded. Knocked down and stunned, he regained consciousness and continued to treat the wounded, reposition his men, and inspire and encourage their efforts. Wounded again when an enemy grenade shattered his left hand, nonetheless he personally took up the fight and armed and threw several grenades which killed a number of enemy soldiers. Seeing that an enemy machine gun had maneuvered behind his platoon and was delivering fire upon his men, Sergeant Morris and another man crawled toward the gun to knock it out. His comrade was killed and Sergeant Morris sustained another wound, but firing his rifle with one hand, he silenced the enemy machine gun. Returning to the platoon, he courageously exposed himself to the devastating enemy fire to drag the wounded to a protected area, and with utter disregard for his personal safety and the pain he suffered, he continued to lead and direct the efforts of his men until relief arrived. Upon termination of the battle, important documents were found among the enemy dead revealing a planned ambush of a Republic of Vietnam battalion. Use of this information prevented the ambush and saved many lives. Sergeant Morris' conspicuous gallantry and intrepidity at the risk of his life above and beyond the call of duty were instrumental in the successful defeat of the enemy, saved many lives, and were in the highest traditions of the United States Army.

Morris receives the Medal of Honor from President Johnson

135

Southerd, Kelley, Morris, Pigeon

It was the first time a soldier under my command had ever been awarded the MOH, and I have so many memories of that time in our lives.

When we finally pushed the enemy back and were sweeping over the position, I walked right by Sgt Morris thinking he was dead. My goal then was to insure that each of the platoons were tied in together, and we were in a position to defend if the enemy were to counterattack. At that moment I heard someone yell, "Morris is alive!"

Returning to where he lay, I knelt down and asked (a really a stupid question), "Sgt Morris, how are you?"

He looked up at me and grabbed my collar, yanking me down towards him he said "Sir, don't let them take me out until the others are lifted out. Don't leave anyone behind."

His concern then, as it had always been, was for the needs of others. I told him that we would get the others out first before we moved him. The reason for this was because I knew he was going to die after suffering the extensive wounds he had.

We got him out on the last lift that evening. But…he didn't die! One year later I was invited to the White House to be present while the President of the United States presented Sgt Morris the Medal of Honor for actions on June 29th; actions that were "above and beyond the call of duty." As great as that was—and for me it was one of the most significant events of my life—I still remember most his words from the year prior, "Sir, don't let 'em take me—don't let them leave anyone behind". Today I remember that the most—and it goes beyond that battlefield as a blessed command. Leave no one behind!

Capt Jack T. Kelley – C.O. of Co A, 2/503rd Airborne Infantry, 173rd Abn Bde.

The Medal of Honor nomination process is governed by a strict set of rules, and packets require the award recommendation, an in-depth narrative, the citation, witness statements and topographical maps with detailed description of the events. The following are verified witness statements by members of the 3rd Platoon. They were taken from the Medal of Honor packet that was presented to the council.

RECOMMENDATION FOR AWARD
OF THE MEDAL OF HONOR

LIST OF ENCLOSURES
   Statement (CPT Conrad N. Walker).
   Statement (SSG Thomas Cooney).
   Statement (PFC Gregg R. Lyell).
   Statement (PFC Thomas S. Shasteen).
   Statement (Edward H. Balls).
   Statement (PFC Michael Sturges).
   Statement (PFC Ivery Robins Jr.).
   Statement (Everet C. Anderson).
   Statement (PFC Leon E. Exum).
   Statement (PFC Jack R. Milner).

DEPARTMENT OF THE ARMY
HEADQUARTERS 2D BATTALION (AIRBORNE) 503D
INFANTRY
APO San Francisco 96250

S-T-A-T-E-M-E-N-T

Sergeant Morris is the most courageous and dedicated soldier
with whom I have ever had the opportunity to serve. He portrays
the highest bearing of combat leadership and example that our
great country has to offer. Even when direly wounded, he
pressed on in such a tenacious way that inspiration and acute
motivation flowed forth with each man in the command. His
refusal to be evacuated prior to the other wounded was an
indescribable display of courage in the battle area. Under this
wondrous character quality in Sergeant Morris, the unit
performed in monumental success in routing a much greater
force. It is a joyous honor to serve with him as his Chaplain.

CONRAD N. WALKER
Captain, Chaplain

DEPARTMENT OF THE ARMY
COMPANY A 2D BATTALION (AIRBORNE) 503D
INFANTRY
APO San Francisco 96250

S-T-A-T-E-M-E-N-T

On 26 June 1966, 1LT Larry Allgood, platoon leader of the 3d platoon of Company A, was wounded from the explosion of a Viet Cong command detonated mine. I, SSG Thomas Cooney, was placed in the position of platoon leader. On 29 June, our company made a heliborne assault on an unprepared landing zone. From the landing zone, my platoon moved out on a search and destroy mission on a separate axis. Realizing my platoon would be operating alone, I had Sergeant Morris take the point with his squad because he was the most dependable NCO I had. Sergeant Morris without doubt is one of the most outstanding NCO's that I have met in my 16 years in the Army. He is a great leader in the NCO Corps, a dedicated soldier, and the most courageous man whom I have had the opportunity to serve with. His drive and enthusiasm left any task assigned him unquestioned. On the morning of 29 June, using Sergeant Morris and his squad as point for the platoon, we took off on the search and destroy mission. If it had not been for Sergeant Morris and his keen sense and alertness in noting several indications of enemy in the area, the results would have been disastrous. Some of the indications were fresh latrines and numerous tire patches used by the Viet Cong to make sandals. I had Sergeant Morris place his men in firing positions and instructed him to check out his front. In so doing, he was fired upon by a .30 caliber machine gun and wounded in the chest. However, he returned fire and knocked out the enemy gun position. He then returned to my location and made a complete and detailed report. He informed me of seeing at least two .50 caliber machine guns, a couple of .30 caliber machine guns, and several mortar positions. I immediately decided to pull back, but as I issued the order the platoon came under a devastating volume of fire and it was then impossible to move. We could only stay and fight and hope for the best. Sergeant Morris quickly moved to his squad under the intense fire. His squad was hardest hit and received heavy casualties. The fire lifted for a short time and the enemy evidently organized themselves for an assault. They came out of their trenches and tried to overrun us, concentrating their efforts towards Sergeant Morris' squad. Even though the squad had already received many casualties, under Sergeant Morris' leadership, they broke the back of the assault. But the enemy did not give up that easy. They made several more attempts to overrun us but Sergeant Morris and the few men he had remaining held them back. During the fighting, Sergeant Morris could be seen moving to and from among his men and could be heard yelling encouragement to them. Before I was seriously wounded and rendered useless, I noted that Sergeant Morris had been hit several times and I ordered him to take time for treatment of his wounds but he refused treatment and continued to fight with his men. He completely disregarded his personal safety throughout the long battle. When the relief force arrived in the area, Sergeant Morris was still painfully dragging himself about, talking to his men and helping to treat their wounds. The heavy fighting ended with the arrival of the relief force but the enemy continued to snipe at us. When the relief force started to evacuate us from the area, I heard Sergeant

Morris say, "Take the others first. They're hurt real bad." Though he was hurt bad himself, he refused to be moved until he knew that all of his men were out. Never have I seen such courage and dedication to our cause. I felt it an honor to have had this man in my platoon and his acquaintance alone makes it a pleasure to serve in the NCO Corps of the United States Army.

Ssg Thomas Cooney
Co A, 2d Bn (Abn) 503d Inf

Sworn to and subscribed before me this 24th day of Sept 1966, at Bien Hoa, Republic of Vietnam.

JACK T. KELLEY
Captain, Infantry
Commanding

DEPARTMENT OF THE ARMY
COMPANY A 2D BATTALION (AIRBORNE) 503D INFANTRY
APO San Francisco 96250

S-T-A-T-E-M-E-N-T

On 29 June 1966 the 3d platoon of Company A ran into a well-entrenched force of Viet Cong. Sergeant Morris was hit while making a recon to our front. He returned to the platoon leader and told him that he had spotted two 50 Cal machine gun positions, two 30 Cal machine gun positions and several mortar positions. Noting that Sergeant Morris had been wounded, the platoon medic offered to patch him up and give him morphine, but he refused by saying there wasn't enough time. When the

141

Viet Cong opened up on us, a 57 mm recoilless rifle was fired at us and exploded in our area. Sergeant Morris was knocked down by several fragments, but got up and moved back to his squad. The enemy fire slacked up some at this point. Sergeant Morris came back looking for the medic but the medic was dead. He then quickly attempted to dress his own wound. The Viet Cong opened up again and Sergeant Morris started to move back to his squad. A grenade fell nearby and he was wounded again. He seemed to be stunned for a few minutes but continued to move forward. During the battle the Viet Cong maneuvered a 50 Cal heavy machine gun to our rear and I saw Sergeant Morris and a wounded man move toward the position. The wounded man was killed and Sergeant Morris was firing into the enemy position when he was wounded by another grenade. He fell behind the body of the dead man and continued firing at the enemy position, which was only a few meters away, until the gun was silenced. Then Sergeant Morris crawled forward to insure that the gun was out of action. I thought it was the most courageous act I have seen in Vietnam.

GREGG R. LYELL
PFC,
Co A, 2d Bn (Abn) 503d Inf

Sworn to and subscribed before me this 8th day of Sept 1966, at Bien Hoa, Republic of Vietnam.

JACK T. KELLEY
Captain, Infantry, Commanding

DEPARTMENT OF THE ARMY
COMPANY A 2D BATTALION (AIRBORNE) 503D INFANTRY
APO San Francisco 96250

S-T-A-T-E-M-E-N-T

On the morning of 29 June our platoon conducted a heliborne assault. We had moved through the jungle for about two hours when we stopped and set up all-around security. Someone had found signs that indicated Viet Cong were in the area. Sergeant Morris went forward to check the area. When the Viet Cong opened up on Sergeant Morris, we knew we were in close proximity to the enemy. Sergeant Morris then returned and briefed the platoon leader on what he had found. He was hit bad at this time. Then all of a sudden the Viet Cong seemed to open up with everything they had. The fighting was heavy for many hours to follow. During the battle, the Viet Cong made several assaults on our position, but we held them off. Sergeant Morris' squad suffered nearly 100% casualties. I heard PFC Marshall yell, "Sarge, I think I just lost my arm." Our medic was already dead, so Sergeant Morris moved to Marshall's position under heavy fire to help him. Marshall had lost an arm and a leg, but Sergeant Morris found a container of Morphine lying in the mud near one of the dead men and after cleaning the needle, injected it into Marshall. PFC Marshall is alive today because of Sergeant Morris' actions. Even though he had been wounded many times himself, Sergeant Morris was eventually evacuated without receiving morphine. There wasn't enough to go around and Sergeant Morris took care of his men first. Throughout the long battle, Sergeant Morris was everywhere, treating the wounded, repositioning men online, redistributing ammo, shouting encouragement. His voice could even be heard above the loud explosions during the heat of the battle. He personally moved all the seriously wounded further to the rear so they would be in a safer position. After the Viet Cong had fled and the fighting was over, I walked to the evacuation LZ where Sergeant Morris was lying beside one of his dead men. I asked if there was anything I could do for him. He replied, "I am alright. I'm hit in quite a few places but I'll be fine." His words gave me new courage as they did to all the men throughout the long fight, because I knew he was hurting more than he would let on. I still wonder how a man can be so courageous and so fearless. He was certainly the most inspiring man I have ever met in my life

THOMAS S. SHASTEEN
PFC,
Co A, 2d Bn (Abn) 503d Inf

Sworn to and subscribed before me this 8th day of Sept 1966, at Bien Hoa, Republic of Vietnam.

JACK T. KELLEY
Captain, Infantry, Commanding

EPARTMENT OF THE ARMY
COMPANY A 2D BATTALION (AIRBORNE) 503D INFANTRY
APO San Francisco 96250

S-T-A-T-E-M-E-N-T

I, PFC Edward H. Balls, was situated amidst the left file of the point squad as we stepped in thick swamp terrain for what appeared to be a rest period after an early morning heliborne assault mission. But we were soon told to be extremely alert because Viet Cong were in the area. At this time Sergeant Morris made a recon to the front and was hit almost immediately. A few minutes after he returned, the Viet Cong opened up on us with heavy and light machine guns, automatic rifle and small arms fire, rifle grenades, mortars and recoilless rifles. The brunt of the heavy explosions occurred amidst the point squad and the CP area. Sergeant Morris disregarded his wounds and fought, instilling courage in his men and setting an example of outstanding combat leadership. Each time I glanced in the direction of Sergeant Morris he was shooting or applying first aid to the wounded within his reach. Under extremely heavy fire, I watched Sergeant Morris crawl from man to man, administering first aid with complete disregard for his own life. Sergeant Morris had been wounded time after time by small arms rounds and grenade fragments in his chest, legs, hands and back. But he continued to lead, aid and encourage his men. He did as he advised us to do, conserved ammo and made each shot count. Sergeant Morris kept a cool head at all times and performed brilliantly under enemy fire with courage above and beyond the call of duty.

PFC EDWARD H. BALLS
Co A, 2d Bn (Abn) 503d Inf

Sworn to and subscribed before me this 8th day of Sept 1966, at Bien Hoa, Republic of Vietnam.

JACK T. KELLEY
Captain, Infantry
Commanding

DEPARTMENT OF THE ARMY
COMPANY A 2D BATTALION (AIRBORNE) 503D
INFANTRY
APO San Francisco 96250

S-T-A-T-E-M-E-N-T

On 29 June 1966 the third platoon encountered a large Viet
Cong force and engaged them in a heavy battle. The point squad
seemed to take the brunt of the attack throughout the battle. We
were receiving many casualties, and I knew we needed
reinforcing. I knew the RTO had been hit. I didn't see or hear
anyone on the radio. I crawled up to the radio, which was up
front. When I arrived up front, the Viet Cong opened fire again.
I looked around and all I saw were bodies lying around with
nobody firing. Then I saw Sergeant Morris up on the line all by
himself looking down his rifle sights. I crawled over to him and
told him he ought to move behind some logs and quit exposing
himself. He asked me to redress the wound on his chest and then
he said he had to take care of his men. Sergeant Morris was the
greatest morale booster I could ever have hoped for. Myself and
some of the others were really beginning to worry because we
had lost all of our leaders. But when we found out that Sergeant
Morris was still going, we got renewed faith. After the battle
was over Sergeant Morris refused to be evacuated until, in his
own words, "the more seriously wounded were out." I talked to
many of the men in the hospital and all they talked about was
the great job Sergeant Morris did. I felt it an honor to serve
under a man with the capabilities and outstanding courage as
Sergeant Morris had.

PFC MICHAEL STURGES
Co A, 2d Bn (Abn) 503d Inf

Sworn to and subscribed before me this 8th day of Sept 1966, at Bien Hoa, Republic of Vietnam.

JACK T. KELLEY
Captain, Infantry
Commanding

DEPARTMENT OF THE ARMY
COMPANY A 2D BATTALION (AIRBORNE) 503D INFANTRY
APO San Francisco 96250

S-T-A-T-E-M-E-N-T

Sergeant Morris was my squad leader on 29 June 1966. When I was fist assigned for service in Vietnam, I was in the communication section of Company A, 2d Bn (Abn) 503d Inf. Then I was assigned to Sergeant Morris' squad where I was received and made to feel like an important and needed individual in the squad. In my experience of serving in this war-torn land, I have never come upon an individual who surpassed Sergeant Morris' military know-how. Because of my experience with him, I think I could never show the man the amount of gratitude and respect which he is most surely due. In the fire fight on 29 June, Sergeant Morris was always where he was needed the most, offering help in every way he could. He really gave his all for his men and his country. His squad was the point squad for the third platoon. When the point man observed freshly dug latrines, Sergeant Morris knew the enemy was close and immediately began to deploy his squad into position. He then moved forward to make a recon. He had moved only a few meters when a six to eight round burst was fired from a light machine gun to our front. I saw Sergeant Morris fall and thought he had been killed. But he raised up and began to fire his rifle into the gun position. He then crawled a few feet forward and threw a grenade into the position. He then crawled out of sight. A few minutes later he returned and saw there were many Viet Cong nearby. Then the Viet Cong opened up with everything they had. We soon sustained heavy casualties. Many of the men were hit bad and Sergeant Morris went to look for the platoon medic. But we later found that our medic had been killed. When Sergeant Morris returned, he did not falter, and despite his wounds, he was giving commands and setting an example of cool-headed self control and courage. He maneuvered himself to aid his men, issued orders and instructions and yelled words of encouragement. He fought with such courage and determination to see his men through the battle that it is a miracle he is alive today. He showed no concern for his personal safety and was a tower of inspiration throughout the long fight.

PFC IVERY ROBINS, Jr..
Co A, 2d Bn (Abn) 503d Inf

Sworn to and subscribed before me this 8th day of Sept 1966, at Bien Hoa, Republic of Vietnam.

JACK T. KELLEY
Captain, Infantry
Commanding

DEPARTMENT OF THE ARMY
COMPANY A 2D BATTALION (AIRBORNE) 503D
INFANTRY
APO San Francisco 96250

S-T-A-T-E-M-E-N-T

On 29 June 1966 Sergeant Morris did an outstanding job throughout the fight. In doing a great job I think Sergeant Morris can be credited for lives saved. All through the fight he crawled around helping the wounded with no concern for his own safety. He moved through heavy enemy fire to get to wounded men. This I saw him do many times and in so doing this I believe he saved many lives. Besides giving first aid, he did very well in keeping up the morale of the entire platoon. Even though he was wounded at various times, he continued to do an outstanding job. On one occasion the Viet Cong shouted, "Die Americans." I heard Sergeant Morris reply, "Come on and fight, cowards." Minutes later he was hit again. He actually tried to draw fire on himself to keep it off the other wounded men. I observed his actions throughout the fight and can honestly say that Sergeant Morris saved many of our lives, perhaps all our lives. In this fire fight, he proved not only to me but to all the other men that were there, what a great soldier he is. He is a man that always acts with total disregard for his own safety in order to accomplish the mission. In return we all owe him a great deal. He is a great leader that we will always remember, especially the ones thatfought beside in on 29 June.

PFC EVERET C. ANDERSON
Co A, 2d Bn (Abn) 503d Inf

Sworn to and subscribed before me this 8th day of Sept 1966, at Bien Hoa, Republic of Vietnam.

JACK T. KELLEY
Captain, Infantry
Commanding

DEPARTMENT OF THE ARMY
COMPANY A 2D BATTALION (AIRBORNE) 503D INFANTRY
APO San Francisco 96250

S-T-A-T-E-M-E-N-T

During the battle on 29 June 1966, Sergeant Morris was wounded several times by small arms fire and grenade fragments. But he never stopped until he finally passed out from loss of blood or exhaustion. We thought he was dead, but after about ten minutes, he started moving again. Because he was wounded so bad, the weapons squad leader tried to get him to lay down, but he refused. The weapons squad leader then tried to hold him down, but Sergeant Morris could not be held. He got up and started to move somewhere. I never knew just where he intended to go. Then the Viet Cong assaulted our position again. They lobbed a grenade in and Sergeant Morris was close to the explosion. I thought it had blown his left hand off. But this didn't seem to even faze him. He began moving up and down the line during the fight in search of more ammo and grenades. He took all he could find from the dead and wounded and distributed it on line. The Viet Cong were right on top of us. Sergeant Morris killed several just a few feet from our lines. Although he had little to no use of his left hand, he continued to fire his weapon and throw grenades. To throw grenades, he held them in his right hand and looped the pin over his left thumb. There didn't seem to be much remaining of his left hand. But Sergeant Morris is one in a million. And he is such a brave man, anyone would be happy to serve under his leadership. He showed no fear toward the enemy. There would have been many more dead today if it weren't for his courage. Never have I seen amore courageous and determined leader of men.

PFC LEON E. EXUM
Co A, 2d Bn (Abn) 503d Inf

Sworn to and subscribed before me this 8th day of Sep 1966, at Bien Hoa, Republic of Vietnam.

RALPH C. SOUTHARD
1LT, Infantry
Executive Officer

DEPARTMENT OF THE ARMY
COMPANY A 2D BATTALION (AIRBORNE) 503D INFANTRY
S-T-A-T-E-M-E-N-T

Sergeant Morris showed me what a real combat sergeant looked like on the battlefield on the 29th of June. His actions were remarkable. I was personally in his squad on that day. Sergeant Morris and PFC Smith got hit while on a recon to our front but Sergeant Morris got Smith back ok. I went and talked to Smith. He said at that time that even though Sergeant Morris was hit much worse than he was that Sergeant Morris stayed out and fought "Charlie" off until he was sure that Smith was safe and then came back in. Then "Charlie" hit us hard, and it looked like we were giving up. So Sergeant Morris started talking to all of us, telling us that "Charlie" was scared of us to, and that if we kept fighting hard and driving on we could make it. His words picked up up the morale of the platoon. After the fight went on for a while many of the men got hit. Sergeant Morris started taking care of them. I looked at him taking care of another fellow and he had blood running from every part of his body. Sergeant Morris never stopped for a moment. He crawled to most all of the positions checking the men. When he was not taking care of the men he was talking on the radio. When he was not talking on the radio he was fighting at the front and keeping the Viet Cong from charging our line. To sum it all up, 1) He was our platoon leader when Sergeant Cooney got hit, 2) He was our medic when the medic got killed, 3) He was our RTO when the RTO got hit, and 4) He was the greatest squad leader I ever saw.

JACK R. MILNER
PFC,
Co A, 2d Bn (Abn) 503d Inf

Sworn to and subscribed before me this 23 day of Sept 1966, at Bien Hoa, Republic of Vietnam.

JACK T. KELLEY
Captain, Infantry
Commanding

~Then and Now~

I'm here again, it's fifty years,
My mind is there this day.
I'm there, like you and all who were,
Who happened by that way.
I sketch now on a cardboard slate
In drizzle, safe and sound,
So different now from how back then
The pencil's words shook like the ground.
I never knew the body count
And never wanted to,
But then we met in retrospect,
And I talked war with you.
I told how I remembered then,
I spoke to you of fearless men,
I spilled the vial that held within
The secrets of a warrior's den,
Where private moments off the sleeve
Are seldom shared by those aggrieve,
And proudly owned as private thought
Could ne'er be stole nor e'er be bought-
These feelings of this band of men
Who hailed from far and wide
To live the war as soldiers did
With loyal warriors by their side.
We few men, our captain says,
Did things we needed do,

153

To leave those woods we left that day
But stay there ever, too,
With those who were our brothers then,
And now, and evermore,
We'll ever hold them, hold them dear,
As we guard freedom's door.

Bubber Fishbourne, PFC Rifleman 1st Platoon
8/2/16

About the Author

Jack was born in Orlando, Florida, July 8, 1937. A member of the Boy Scouts of America, he was awarded the Eagle Scout badge. He graduated from the Citadel in 1959 and was commissioned as a 2d Lt of Infantry in the US Army. In November 1977, he retired from the U.S. Army as a Lt. Col., after twenty years of service. He commanded parachute infantry units at platoon, company, and battalion levels where his last two assignments were as a Battalion Commander in the 82nd

Airborne Division and finally, as Deputy Commander, 5th Special Forces ("Green Berets"). Jack was awarded the Silver Star for gallantry in action, the Legion of Merit, the Distinguished Flying Cross, the Bronze Star Medal with "V" device for Valor with six oak leaf clusters, the Purple Heart, Meritorious Service Medal, Air Medal – eleventh Award, Joint Service Commendation Medal, and Army Commendation Medal with two oak leaf clusters. He also was awarded the Combat Infantryman's Badge, the Expert Infantryman's Badge Senior Parachutist Badge, Pathfinder Badge, and the Aircrew Badge, the Army Staff and Joint Staff Identification Badges.

He has earned Master's Degrees from both American University and Central Michigan, served as a Certified Financial Planner (CFP), and as an Adjunct Professor at both Webster University and Campbell University. Jack served as the Executive Director of Men's Ministries of the Pentecostal Holiness Church (IPHC), a position he held from 1985 to 2005 and was one of the founders of Men's Ministries IPHC. In 2006 he was awarded the Lifetime Achievement Award from the National Coalition of Men's Ministries (NCMM). NCMM is a network of denominational and para-church ministries, which represents more than half of the churches in the United States, and the Commander Bill Linn Award from the Royal Ranger Ministry (IPHC) for shaping the lives of boys. He also served as the Vice President of Advancement/Director of Development for Holmes Bible College.

The All American Airborne Awards organization recognized him as the 173rd Airborne Brigade Association Man of the Year. In June 2016 he was recognized by the Secretary of the Army as a Distinguished Member of the 503rd Infantry (Airborne) Regiment. He is currently a member of the Bragg Chapter of the Military Order of the Purple Heart.

Jack and his wife, Lynn are members of Northwood Temple Church where he was ordained and served on the church staff for five years. From 1985 to 2005 he served as the Director of Men's Ministries of his denomination-the International Pentecostal Holiness Church. Since then he has been a volunteer for the Military Order of the Purple Heart. The Kelley's live in Fayetteville, N.C. Telephone:(c) 910-978-8777 Jack's email is: JackTKelley@aol.com

Glossary

Term	Description
292 Antenna	Antenna-An elevated, wide band, ground plane antenna designed to increase the range of our PRC-10 radios. Receptions increased to over 8 miles from our normal PRC - 10 antenna. The 292 weighed 48 lbs and was able to allow us a mast of 30 feet.
105mm How	A large cannon that combines the velocity of a gun with the high trajectory firing capability of a mortar.
81mm Mortars	81mm smooth bore high angle infantry mortar. Three basic rounds could be used: HE high explosive-range 5,180, WP white phosphorus angle 4,934 and Ill-illumination-burns for 75 seconds with range of 1,200 yards illuminating an area of 1,200 yards.
AA	After Action Report
AK-47	A Soviet-made, gas operated 7.62mm assault rifle. Inexpensive and easily maintained.
AO	Area of Operations
ARVN	Army of the Republic of Vietnam
ARCOM	US military decoration – Army Commendation Medal
Body Bag	Plastic bags used for retrieval of bodies on the battlefield.
Bronze Star	US military decoration

C-4	A very stable plastic explosive carried by infantry soldiers. Easy and light to carry, also stable and a potent explosive, malleable with texture similar to play dough, it would be formed into shaped charges of infinite configurations. Would not explode without a detonator device. Used also in mechanical ambushes, along with claymores, etc.
COSVN	Central Office of South Vietnam (People's Army of Vietnam)
CSM	Command Sergeant Major
Dust Off	Medical evacuation helicopter. On June 29 they consisted of HUEY 1-D, Chinooks, Air Force Medical helicopters, as well as regular HUEY's that lowered a rope to evacuate the wounded and dead.
Duty Officer	The officer at battalion level that was manning the command radios and records in all traffic received from the company's below or from higher headquarters- He maintained the Battalion Log-recording those transactions.
FDC	Fire Direction Center is in the artillery unit supporting the infantry unit fighting – the FDC calculated adjustments of cannon fire to cause the shells to impact on target. Our FDC was in A Battery, 3d Battalion of the 319th Airborne Artillery Regiment.
Fields of Fire	Military terminology that describes a weapon's ability to cover a given area.

FO	Forward Observer – Forward Observer travels with the infantry company and coordinates artillery missions, to include coordinating the fires of night defensive positions.
Grenades	Fragmentation-M61-developed to be effective for close in combat, the M61 is a high yield limited range grenade. Effective casualty radius was 15 meters. The M61 uses two separate arming actions, pulling the pin and releasing the jungle clip prior to throwing the grenade, grenade with a 4-5 second delay after the handles fry off. Can be thrown for 125 feet by average soldier.
KIA	Killed In Action
LAW	The M-72 LAW was essentially a two-piece weapon, with one piece sliding within the other. Fully extended with weapons fired its 66 mm rocket propelled war head capable of defeating armor and concrete fortifications of the day. Its round was called a HEAT round. It weighed about 5 pounds and because of the weight, the operator was able to carry several. Once fired, the weapon was useless and had to be destroyed to keep it from being used by the enemy for booby traps. In our battle it was very effective in destroying enemy bunkers.
LFT	Light Fire Team- helicopters
LZ	Landing Zone

M-16	Select-fire, 5.56 rifle with a 20 round magazine.
M18 Claymore Mines	A command-denotated, antipersonnel mine which is capable of throwing a shower of shrapnel at the enemy force.
M60	The M-60 machine gun weighed a little over 23 pounds, was gas operated with a 50-round link belt of 7.62 mm ammo. It would fire 100 rounds per minute, with a max effective range of 1,200 yards – with bipod an additional 329 feet.
M-79	A single hot shoulder-fired weapon break-action grenade launcher. Can fire a variety of 40mm rounds including explosives, anti-personnel, smoke, and buckshot among others.
MASH	Mobile Army Surgical Hospital. The Vietnam war was radically different from the Korean War and drastic changes in combat philosophy were needed. Though MASH is a common term where we were, there are other terms that were more accurate - for example, the 3rd Surgical Hospital in Bien Hoa was a semi-permanent field medical facility and the 45th Surgical a MUST unit (Medical Unit Self Contained was an expandable, mobile with expandable inflated ward sections.

NARA	National Archives Records Administration is an independent agency of the United

	Stated Government charged with preserving documents and historical records. It increases public access to those documents which comprise the National Archives.
NPAC	National Personnel Records Center
NVA	North Vietnamese Army
OPORD	Operations Orders
Pistol	M1911A-A single action, semi-automatic, magazine fed, recoil operated pistol chambered for the .45 ACP cartridge.
PTL	Praise The Lord
Purple Heart	US military decoration awarded for wounds received by enemy action.
Recon	(a) a term to indicate a movement to seek out the enemy of (b) to describe a mission of the Battalion Reconnaissance Platoon.
Release Points (RP)	Points designated where the Platoon Leaders, once reached and authorized, where on their own to commence their own search and destroy movement to the objective.
RPG	Rocket Propelled Grenade. A shoulder-fired portable, anti-tank weapons system. Designed by the Soviets.
RTO	Radio Telephone Operator
Scorched Earth	A military strategy that targets anything that might be useful to the enemy while it is advancing through or withdrawing from a location...examples -food sources, water supplies, transportation, and communications.

Silver Star	US decoration for gallantry in action
Stand To	That period of time both at dawn and twilight, just as the light is beginning or decreasing and was a favorable time for an enemy attack. At that time the unit would go to "stand to" which meant-full alert, weapons being checked, fields of fire being observed and, familiarization with those standard operating procedures of calling in artillery or firing the defensive claymores implanted.
Walk the Line	A task that leaders of small units perform in order to check on their soldiers.
WIA	Wounded In Action

To order additional copies or to request for more information, please contact the author at: JackTKelley@aol.com